PRAISE FOR

The Problem of Twelve

"Capitalism is determined by who controls capital. John Coates draws on a lifetime of experience and study to make a compelling case that American capitalism part way into the twenty-first century is dominated by a dozen insufficiently accountable institutions. His pathbreaking analysis and recommendations deserve the attention of all who care about our economic future."

LAWRENCE H. SUMMERS
Frank and Denie Weil Director of the Mossavar-Rahmani
Center for Business and Government, Charles W. Eliot
University Professor, Harvard Kennedy School

"In this concise but broad-ranging exposition of how index funds and private equity funds are changing the nature of American capitalism, John Coates unpacks the complex economic and political effects of these financial intermediaries. He offers some sensible first steps in what he explains will be the long-term challenge of containing their negative effects without losing the substantial benefits that index funds, in particular, have produced for American households."

DANIEL K. TARULLO
Nomura Professor of International
Financial Regulatory Practice at Harvard Law School
and former member of the Federal Reserve Board

"The political dangers arising from concentrated economic power are a recurrent theme in American history. Coates's book provides an essential tutorial on the influence of a small number of private financial institutions, and the answers needed for our own reckoning with concentrated financial power."

TIM WU
author of *The Curse of Bigness*, former special assistant
to President Biden for technology and competition policy

The Problem of Twelve
When a Few Financial Institutions Control Everything

COLUMBIA GLOBAL REPORTS
NEW YORK

The Problem of Twelve

When a Few Financial Institutions Control Everything

John Coates

Published by Columbia Global Reports
91 Claremont Avenue, Suite 515
New York, NY 10027
globalreports.columbia.edu
facebook.com/columbiaglobalreports
@columbiaGR

Library of Congress Cataloging-in-Publication Data

Names: Coates, John, 1948- author.
Title: The problem of twelve : when a few financial institutions control
    everything / John Coates.
Description: New York, NY : Columbia Global Reports, [2023] | Includes
    bibliographical references.
Identifiers: LCCN 2023011803 (print) | LCCN 2023011804 (ebook) |
    ISBN 9798987053546 (paperback) | ISBN 9798987053553 (ebook)
Subjects: LCSH: Financial institutions. | Index mutual funds. | Private equity.
Classification: LCC HG4523 .C623 2023 (print) | LCC HG4523 (ebook) |
    DDC 332.06--dc23/eng/20230424
LC record available at https://lccn.loc.gov/2023011803
LC ebook record available at https://lccn.loc.gov/2023011804

Book design by Strick&Williams
Map design by Jeffrey L. Ward
Author photograph by Martha Stewart

Printed in the United States of America

CONTENTS

Index fund: A type of mutual fund that pools investments from dispersed individuals and institutions and invests in all companies in a specified "index" or list, usually chosen by a third party, such as the S&P 500 index

> **BlackRock:** Largest asset manager in the world, the bulk of the assets of which are invested through index funds, one of the "Big Four" index fund providers

> **Vanguard:** Pioneer of index funds and now one of the largest asset managers in the world, one of the "Big Four" index fund providers

> **State Street:** Multiline bank that pioneered index-based "exchange traded funds," such as iShares, one of the "Big Four" index fund providers

> **Fidelity:** Large asset manager, traditionally associated with actively managed funds, but now increasingly managing assets in index funds, one of the "Big Four" index fund providers

Public company: A business whose owners are hundreds or thousands or millions of dispersed individuals and institutions, required to be registered with the SEC and to make regular disclosures to the public

SEC: Securities and Exchange Commission, the primary federal agency overseeing public companies and index funds

Mutual fund: A collective method of investing, sponsored by a fund advisor, that sells shares to the public, promises to redeem those shares at any time based on the net asset value of the fund, and uses its funds to invest in varying assets, such as public company stock, required to be registered with the SEC and required to make regular disclosures to the public

Exchange traded fund: A collective method of investing that is usually economically similar to index mutual funds but structured somewhat differently for legal and tax purposes, also required to be registered with the SEC

Private equity fund: A collective method of investing that focuses on buying, holding, and selling whole companies, usually raising money primarily from institutional investors, called "private" because they limit

ownership in such a way as to not require registration with the SEC as a
public company or a mutual fund, and as a result are not required to make
public disclosures

KKR: A major private equity fund sponsor, famous for the RJR Nabisco
leveraged buyout in 1989 (then the largest such buyout in history), now
itself a public company but sponsoring multiple private equity funds

Blackstone: A major private equity fund sponsor, itself now a public
company but sponsoring multiple private equity funds

Carlyle: A major private equity fund sponsor, itself now a public company but sponsoring multiple private equity funds

Apollo: A major private equity fund sponsor, itself now a public company but sponsoring multiple private equity funds

Junk bond: Any "fixed income" (i.e., debt) security that is not rated "investment grade" (highly rated) by a credit rating agency, typically riskier than
other kinds of bonds, commonly used in leveraged buyouts

Introduction

A "problem of twelve"[*] arises when a small number of actors acquires the means to exert outsized influence over the politics and economy of a nation. In US history, problems of twelve have recurred, as the result of a clash of two fundamental forces: economies of scale in finance on the one hand, and constitutional commitments to fragmented and limited political power on the other. Each time, the "problem" has been two-sided. The concentration of wealth and power in a small number of hands threatens the political system and the people generally, and the political response can threaten the financial institutions in which wealth and power are accumulating, even when those institutions create economic benefits.

Today, two late-twentieth century institutions—index funds and private equity funds—are creating a new problem of twelve. As financial organizations, they amass and invest capital, and have been primarily scrutinized through a financial

[*] "Twelve" is a notional number—the precise number is simply a small one.

lens. As with other financial institutions, they pool savings from dispersed individuals and channel it to fund major projects. They facilitate capitalism, which has created huge benefits for humanity—wealth, health, and much longer life spans—along with inequality, misery, and the existential threat of climate change. Finance creates value by facilitating change, but distributes the gains unequally, and magnifies the gales of "creative destruction."

But both kinds of funds are now so large, and have influence over so much of the economy, that they have economic and political power, whether they want it or not. Their power makes them targets of political threats. Both institutions exhibit "economies of scale." Both are active politically—directly, and indirectly—through their control of businesses.

Their growing and concentrated wealth and power threatens the foundations of a democratic republic built on Montesquieu's separation of powers as well as federalism—the "checks and balances" taught to every civics student. In a predictable response, the republic is increasingly threatening each type of institution with new restrictions, burdens, and limits. Because index funds certainly, and private equity funds possibly, create value within the US economy, the threats to them are as important as their potential threats to American democracy.

The book proceeds as follows. Chapter one notes prior problems of twelve—those created by central banks, private banks, insurance companies, and "money trusts." It summarizes how policy responses to those problems left the dominant form of US business—large companies owned by dispersed investors—in control of their executives, with weak public legitimacy and accountability, as diagnosed in 1932 by Adolf

14   Berle and Gardiner Means. Chapter one also reviews ways that the law and policy restored the legitimacy of those companies, and hence of capitalism, from the depths of the Great Depression: directly with securities law and disclosure requirements, and indirectly with labor law, taxation, and regulation.

Chapter two reviews the emergence of index funds in the last decades of the twentieth century, and analyzes their growing scale and influence. Core parts of the story include a revolution in financial theory, the slow diffusion of a powerful investing idea, and the ways that index funds have managed to exert increasing influence on large businesses, despite being heavily regulated in ways that include extensive disclosure requirements and prohibitions on exerting direct control over companies.

Chapter three describes the transformation of the limited and controversial buyout firms of the 1970s and 1980s into the massive and ever-expanding "private equity" industry of today. Core parts of the private equity story also start with finance theory and innovation, but, unlike index funds, private equity firms have engaged in persistent and largely successful political and public relations efforts to keep the public in the dark about how they operate and restructure companies they control. I also explain the ways that private equity has over time become more complex and permanent as a form of ownership and control over businesses. The chapter ends with a review of the limited research on whether private equity provides net economic benefits to investors, and of its potential for inflicting harm on others.

Chapter four lays out the political side of the problem of twelve that each of these types of funds creates. The largely

successful efforts by business lobbies to shed the limits of labor
law, taxation, and regulation during the last twenty years of the
twentieth century were coupled with new economic challenges,
including globalization, technology, and inflation. The results—
hostile takeovers, buyouts, and the emergence of a powerful
new institutional shareholder movement, all accompanied by
falling public trust in business—are important parts of the current political landscape, in which index funds and private equity
funds are feared, and threatened.

I then review the political activities and influence of index
and private equity funds. Index funds already face limits on
their power, are more likely to vote in line with retail investors
than with other institutions, and are more varied in their political positions than is typically appreciated. Private equity funds,
by contrast, are drawing a veil over more sectors of the economy,
leveraging politically controversial tax breaks, continuing the
suppression of labor and increasing wealth disparities, and
being excellent at whatever private for-profit business they
do—whether increasing productivity or imposing social costs.
The chapter includes specific examples of the kinds of political
threats each type of fund poses and faces.

The book ends in chapter five by asking: What can be done?
What kinds of policy responses might contain these new problems of twelve? Can we reduce the political and policy risks that
each institution creates, without reducing the economic benefits they create? My analysis and answers are tentative—the
choices involved are matters of judgment. Yet it is clear that
some blunt responses, particularly those involving index funds,
will require a higher price in the form of economic losses than
further blunting the political influence of index funds justifies.

16   Others—those involving more disclosure requirements, and some form of public consultation—seem likely to be beneficial. In between are other ideas worth exploring: more vigorous application of antitrust law to the companies each type of fund owns; more robust application of conflict-of-interest rules, not just to the funds but also to their advisors and affiliates; and articulation and enforcement of fiduciary obligations, not simply to investors, but to the broader public these funds affect.

What Came Before

The Twentieth Century's Public Company

The current problem of twelve is new. But it echoes—in a more extreme form—problems that have arisen before. To appreciate what the problem is, why it has arisen, and how we might cope with it, we need a picture of what came before. This chapter reviews how the US economy came to be dominated in the twentieth century by what is called "the public company." Public companies are large businesses with shares traded on a stock exchange. Examples are household names: Apple, AT&T, Costco, Exxon, IBM. Roughly 70 to 80 percent of all corporate ownership has for over a hundred years consisted of public companies' shares.

There is a deep, structural conflict between American-style democratic republicanism, on the one hand, and capitalist economics, particularly in finance, on the other. Democracy as practiced in the US has from the founding been suspicious of, and has imposed legal and political control over, any kind of concentrated power. Capitalist markets often generate economies of scale in finance, which tends to concentrate wealth and

18   power. The result is a repeated pattern of evolution toward concentration, followed by political reaction and the embrace of
laws and institutions that effectively sacrifice some economic
value to thwart the risk of tyranny.

Public companies in the early twentieth century had many
qualities—both good and bad—that today also characterize
the funds that create the problem of twelve: size; growth; concentration; economic dominance; political influence; limited
transparency, legitimacy, and accountability; and accidental
governance. Many of these features also characterize major
financial institutions—banks, "money trusts," and insurance
companies. These institutions are also often public companies,
and have also generated large political conflict in US history.
The result of those conflicts are enduring structural laws bar-
ring those institutions from playing major roles in controlling
or governing other public companies. This helped pave the way
for the problem of twelve created by index funds and private
equity funds.

Public companies are legally overseen by boards of directors, who are formally elected by shareholders. In smaller companies, these formalities map onto reality—a small group of
shareholders effectively control board elections, and, through
them, the companies. This is the way corporate law and governance were designed to function. But in the largest public companies, shareholders have long been so numerous—no one
person owns more than 1 percent of a company's shares—that
contested elections of directors are rare. Because board members are typically independent and serve part-time, they have
limited ability to direct managers. While boards grew in power
at the end of the twentieth century, they still impose only mild

constraints on executives. As a result, large public companies for most of the twentieth century were controlled not by their owners but by their executives. This fact was first highlighted in a 1932 book by Adolf Berle and Gardiner Means, *The Modern Corporation and Private Property*.

For most of the last century, power in public companies— and so in the overall economy—was achieved through a professional career in management: typically, an MBA from a business school, an entry-level management job, and steady progress within a corporate hierarchy. Overall, managerial success blended meritocracy, occasional nepotism, and organizational politics. In sum, the US economy became "managerialist," a mode of separated ownership and control that carried it through what Henry Luce called "the American Century."

Managerialism was an accidental by-product of two forces, one economic, one legal and political: first, the economies of scale produced by the revolutions in production, transportation, and communication of the nineteenth century, and second, laws inhibiting large banks from emerging in the US, and which barred equally large insurance companies (which did emerge) from owning public companies' stock.

The problem of twelve, then, is largely about the threat in the present moment posed by index funds and private equity funds to a class of American corporate managers, and to the economy they have dominated for a hundred years. To set the stage for how the problem of twelve emerged, this chapter briefly reviews how and why managerialism emerged, how it was controlled, and how it achieved enough legitimacy to endure for a century.

20   Adolf Berle and Gardiner Means

While concentration of power and wealth associated with ever-larger companies attracted pushback in the form of anti-trust law beginning in the 1880s, the basic fact of dispersed ownership went unaddressed until as late as 1933, the year Franklin Roosevelt became president and the New Deal began. The largest corporations came to be seen as illegitimate and unaccountable, serving neither social ends nor the private interests of their shareholders. The dispersion of ownership was enabling an increase in concentration of wealth and power—not within banks or insurance companies, as in the past, but in public companies themselves.

Adolf Berle and Gardiner Means observed that the "means of production" (they were using Karl Marx's phrase) in the US economy were becoming concentrated in the hands of the largest two hundred corporations. This, they argued, was a problem—not quite a problem of twelve, but a problem none-theless. "Economic power in the hands of the few persons," as Berle and Means put it,

> can harm or benefit a multitude of individuals, affect whole districts, shift the currents of trade, bring ruin to one community and prosperity to another. The organiza-tions which they control have passed far beyond the realm of private enterprise—they have become more nearly social institutions.

In effect, large public companies were becoming stronger than government. Their dominance made it important to identify who controlled them, and how they were controlled.

Berle and Means were the first systematically to argue that 21
public companies were supervised not by their owners, as
property had been in the past, but by professional managers,
who tended to own little stock in the companies. This theme of
the "separation of ownership and control" is the enduring contribution of Berle and Means to understanding how large businesses function.

Although the Berle-Means critique has been itself criticized
as overstated, it had enormous influence on how companies were
understood, both at the time and since. Its influence derived in
part from its having been an extension of ideas from decades of
muckraking journalistic attacks on the Robber Barons of the
Gilded Age, the wars between trusts and trust-busters, and the
prior political battles against centralized finance. Progressive
thought leaders had already noted the dangers implied by economic scale. Louis Brandeis attacked "bigness" in all its forms,
and as early as 1914 he was recommending sunlight (disclosure)
as the best disinfectant for the resulting ills of corruption and
waste.

The stock market crash of 1929 reinforced these critiques.
The crash revealed widespread fraud and unified the public and
elected officials in demanding reform. As Joel Seligman notes,
"[w]ithin ten weeks of the . . . crash, six members of Congress
introduced bills to regulate corporate financial statements,
margin loans, or short sales of securities." In the longer market
slide from 1930 into 1931, "the flurry of bills introduced were
not just the hastily drawn creations of relatively obscure junior
members," but were led by "Virginia's Carter Glass, . . . [a] life-
long conservative, . . . [who] generally opposed 'centralized'
federal power . . . [b]ut [whose] conservatism permitted one

22   consistent exception . . . the application of federal controls
against the New York City 'money crowd.'" In business historian
Thomas McGraw's retelling, "By 1933, . . . there was obvious
need to restore buyers' confidence. Everyone in the securities
industry knew . . . that something must be done."

Highly publicized congressional investigations, supervised
by Ferdinand Pecora, from 1932 to 1934—patterned after similar
hearings about insurance companies and "money trusts" from
earlier in the century—revealed rampant corporate abuse. As
Ron Chernow writes, "Pecora had charts showing that Morgan
partners held 126 directorships in 89 corporations with $20 bil-
lion in assets. He later called this 'incomparably the greatest
reach of power in private hands in our entire history.'" The Great
Depression destroyed, in the minds of most Americans, whatever legitimacy prior economic growth had produced for public
companies.

In large part, the legitimacy that public companies eventually achieved owes much to Franklin Roosevelt's embrace of a
regime of "full and fair disclosure" in 1933, and in 1934 the creation of the Securities and Exchange Commission (SEC) to
instantiate that regime. The SEC enacted and enforced rules for
public companies, requiring them to publish annual reports, to
pay for independent audits, and to embrace better governance
in the form of rules for how dispersed shareholders could vote,
and with what information. These changes were real, salient,
and publicized.

Together, the sunlight these laws shone on public companies helped restore confidence, not only in the companies
themselves, and eventually in capital markets, but in the entire

American economy. Confidence was restored not only for investors but for the broader public as well. The new laws improved
on preexisting corporate law to help make executives more
accountable to shareholders—to restore a greater degree of
power and control to those who invested capital, and so who
bore the most risk and had the greatest claim to owning the
companies.

Transparency to dispersed owners inevitably also meant
transparency to the public. With that transparency came greater
assurance that companies were actually engaged in sales of
valuable products and services and were not simply engines for
private corruption or concentration of power.

It's evidence of the importance of the SEC's creation and its
initial agenda that they were initially resisted by corporate
managers, who attacked them as "Russian" (meaning commu-
nist). The SEC's start-up period met massive resistance in specific areas—particularly from the stock exchanges, whose
power in the capital markets had only increased in the twenties,
and from public utilities, which had the worst features of
Berle-Means size, ownership dispersion, economic concentration, and insulation from accountability. Yet after a fraught
transitional decade, the constraints of SEC rules came to be
accepted by most business leaders, however grudgingly, as rem-
edies for the global economic ills of the Depression that were far
milder than the alternatives of fascism or socialism.

It is sometimes forgotten that American socialism—so
often emphasized as a dire threat to freedom during the Cold
War—remained a live option in the US through World War II.
As late as 1942, the Roper-Fortune poll found that 25 percent

24   felt that "some form of socialism would be a good thing . . . for the country as a whole." Public companies, after all, were large, autonomous organizations with massive power and no account-ability to the broader publics they nevertheless dominated. During the Depression, they were not easily defended as eco-nomically better than state-owned enterprises, and the latter had the virtue of being managed by people accountable to dem-ocratically elected officials.

The SEC's new disclosure regime provided a reason to believe that privately owned public companies could better achieve economic goals than their state-owned potential coun-terparts. In fact, securities regulation provided companies with benefits beyond restored political legitimacy. By forcing com-panies to be open about risks and to account for their activities, and by helping create safe securities trading markets, SEC rules led investors to be willing to provide companies with capital at a lower price than in other developed economies. Capital markets deepened, and became more liquid, as a result of SEC oversight, further reducing the cost of capital. Cheaper and more liquid capital, in turn, helped companies to grow, to generate jobs, and to distribute wealth among a large class of workers and inves-tors. US capital markets remain the largest and deepest in the world, in large part due to the SEC.

From the 1930s to the 1980s, a typical Berle-Means-style US public company went through a fairly standard life cycle, consisting of three phases of capital raising and governance.

In the first stage, entrepreneurs created companies with capital from some mix of savings, speculative investment from "family, friends, and fools," and, for many companies from the

1950s on, from venture capital firms. Securities law imposed hard and clear caps on the number of investors that could have their personal wealth swept by mania or fraud into these companies, while the companies remained fully private. Many would fail, but the impact of failure was confined and investors were presumed to be able to look out for themselves.

In the second stage, after getting a business to the stage where it was generating revenue and appeared sustainable, an entrepreneur would take the firm public in an initial public offering—that is, sell shares to dispersed, anonymous investors, and list the stock on a stock exchange. Investors obtained shares that were salable on a secondary market, as well as the protections of mandatory audits, disclosure, and oversight by the SEC.

The process of any public offering was tightly regulated, with bans on certain kinds of promotional activity such as billboards and television. Various gatekeepers—underwriters, auditors, and lawyers—would help assure investors that they were being told all there was to know about the company's prospects and risks. No one investor would buy a controlling position, and few would own more than 5 percent of the shares.

In the third stage—with ownership separated from control, and dispersed investors rationally ignorant and passive—any external harms public companies might inflict on anyone other than their shareholders were kept in check by the large body of law and regulation created by the New Deal and the labor unions they empowered. No one manager or group of managers controlled more than one large public company, and antitrust law largely prevented the domination of any industry by any one

26   company. Individual public companies might be large and powerful, and their managers largely autonomous, but they were not part of a dense network of centralized or coordinated financial power, and they clashed as much as they aligned in the political sphere.

The Rise of Index Funds and the Problem of Twelve

The American corporate governance system sketched out in chapter one is dying. Two new types of institutions—index funds and private equity funds—have increasingly and persistently begun to disrupt the public company model. Index funds are investment vehicles for both ordinary people and big institutions: you give them your money, and they try to replicate the overall performance of the stock markets, while charging you only minimal fees. Private equity funds, whose investors are mostly institutions, buy a controlling ownership in companies, often taking them off of the public markets, and then resell them a few years later. These have been by far the fastest growing types of ownership of companies over the last generation.

The subjects of this chapter—index funds—have proven to be such a successful method for ordinary Americans to invest that they have grown continuously since the early 1970s, with a sustained takeoff since 2000, acquiring so much stock that

28 they threaten to overshadow managers at large public companies. Index funds have now gathered so much capital and concentrated so much ownership that they have enough voting power to strongly influence, if not determine, how public companies are governed. Corporate managerialism is threatening to give way to index fund managerialism. No longer do we have an economy controlled by thousands of executive managers of thousands of public companies, held in check by an array of dispersed governance institutions. Instead, we increasingly have an economy overseen by a concentrated collection of roughly a dozen index fund managers, who collectively have enough corporate power to determine the fate of most public companies. This is the first problem of twelve.

As an illustration of the power of index funds, consider the 2021 proxy battle between ExxonMobil and a start-up climate impact investing hedge fund called Engine No. 1. It looked like a classic David and Goliath battle. ExxonMobil had more than $300 billion of assets, while Engine No. 1 (named after one of San Francisco's oldest firehouses) had just been founded by a hedge fund veteran named Chris James, seeded with $250 million of his own funds. Despite owning only 0.02 percent of the company's shares, Engine No. 1 announced it was going to seek to replace four members of ExxonMobil's board of directors. Not many people gave the effort much chance of success: fewer than half of attempts by outside shareholders to replace existing board members have succeeded in recent years, and such campaigns face even longer odds when the shareholder owns a small stake and when the public company being targeted is large.

Yet to the shock of all—almost certainly to the board of ExxonMobil—Engine No. 1 won three seats at ExxonMobil's shareholder meeting on May 26, 2021. What made the outcome especially striking was that Engine No. 1 had not campaigned primarily on the basis of traditional activist themes—that ExxonMobil was performing poorly, or that it could engage in some type of financial restructuring that would unlock shareholder value—although poor performance was part of Engine No. 1's message. Rather, the central talking point was about climate's financial risks for the company: ExxonMobil was not going green fast enough, in the face of rising financial risks from climate change—both physical risks and, more importantly for an oil and gas company, "transition risks"—the risk that public policy would rapidly shift energy fundamentals toward sustainable sources and leave ExxonMobil behind. Engine No. 1's nominees included not only a petroleum marketing executive and strategist from Google, but also a sustainability executive from a petroleum refining and marketing company and the CEO of a wind turbine power company. Even before the contested vote, Exxon pledged to add a director with sustainable investing experience to its board in an attempt to blunt Engine No. 1's message.

For our purposes, what's important is that the votes of two prominent index funds significantly contributed to Engine No. 1's success. Larry Fink, the CEO of the largest index fund company, BlackRock, which controls $10 trillion in assets, had made repeated public comments indicating that his firm would be expecting the companies in which it invested to do more to take account of the long-run risks of their activities, especially from climate change. The ExxonMobil vote was an important marker to show that Fink's words were not cheap talk, but backed by action. Even more surprising was the vote by Vanguard, which

30   has more than $8 trillion in assets. Vanguard, in contrast to both BlackRock and State Street (the third of the Big Three index fund advisors, with more than $4 trillion in assets), had been more circumspect in its public commitments to activism of any kind. Yet Vanguard, too, voted in favor of Engine No. 1's nominees.

How Index Funds Emerged

During the 1960s and early 1970s, in publications by MIT management professor Paul Cootner, Princeton economist Burton G. Malkiel, Chicago economist Eugene Fama, and MIT economist Paul Samuelson, academic researchers advanced several bold ideas—still counterintuitive to many:

- Stock prices reflect all available information—the "efficient market hypothesis."
- As a result, stock prices follow an unpredictable "random walk."
- The best overall method for investing by ordinary individual investors would be to give their savings to funds that would not try to predict the market, but simply to buy and hold a preset basket of stocks.

Samuelson's work drew on the much earlier but largely overlooked 1900 PhD thesis, called "The Theory of Speculation," by French mathematician Louis Bachelier. Roughly at the same time as Malkiel's and Samuelson's work, the same approach was used by Chicago economists Fischer Black and Myron Scholes and MIT economist Robert Merton to develop the still-standard model of how to price options on stock and other assets.

The upshot of this academic theorizing was that a business   31
case could be made for mutual funds to commit to remaining
truly passive. By remaining inactive, the academics argued, the
funds could dramatically reduce their own costs. They could
just invest in a third-party "index" of companies—not in one, or
a set, but in all of them—and they could do so in a fixed way,
based (for example) on simply allocating capital based on the
market value of the stock of the companies in the index.

Through the 1980s, however, this research only made a
modest impact beyond academics. Funds remained active in the
sense of hiring financial professionals at significant expense
who would try to pick winners and losers from among public
companies. Mutual funds did not rapidly take over the retail
investment market. Many people continued to hold shares
directly, and while fund growth was steady, it was slow. Mutual
funds became important but not dominant owners (even in
aggregate) of public companies.

Building directly on this academic revolution in finance
theory, Jack Bogle, who had recently been fired by the Wellington
Fund, made the bold move to found The Vanguard Group in
1974. Vanguard in 1976 created the First Index Investment
Trust, a precursor to the Vanguard 500 Index Fund, as the first
index mutual fund available to the general public. Promising the
lowest advisory fees in the industry, Vanguard committed itself
to giving up on actively picking and choosing stocks, or indeed
to doing much of anything as an institutional investor. Instead,
it would take funds invested by its own investors and simply
buy and hold all the shares in an index of stocks chosen by a
third party.

32   Vanguard's bold new idea for asset management was not, it is fair to say, an immediate hit. Indeed, it was derided on Wall Street. People called the fund "Bogle's Folly." Fifty years later, Vanguard's funds own more equity in US public companies than any individual or organization in US history, closely rivaled only by another index fund complex, BlackRock, which is the world's largest asset manager. In 2005, Paul Samuelson equated Bogle's innovation with the wheel, the alphabet, and the Gutenberg press. Perhaps a financial economist may be forgiven for exaggerating the overall importance to humanity of the index fund, but it is undoubtedly one of the top financial innovations in world history. And as Bogle himself acknowledged shortly before his death in 2019, Vanguard is at the core of the problem of twelve.

The Case for Indexed Investing

How do the arcane components of the financial revolution summarized above translate into a real-world case for indexed investing? Stating the case for index funds is also an important foundation for considering the policy dilemma raised by the problem of twelve—how important is it that index funds be preserved as an option for individual investors?

The basic pitch for index funds is they are a cost-effective way for individual Americans to invest in broadly diversified portfolios, especially for the 99 percent of the population who lack the wealth required to hire a full-time and trusted personal financial advisor. Index funds provide better risk-adjusted returns than if such investors tried to invest directly in public company stocks, and on average better than investing through other institutional channels. It is not true that no one can beat

the market. Many professionals can in fact generate added value
for their investment clients—that is, they can select or weight
stocks to achieve greater returns than if they simply invested in
standard indexes.

The problem for individual investors, however, is that they
cannot easily identify, or identify at all, which financial professionals can beat the market and which cannot. It is hard even for
expert researchers to do that after the fact. A professional's
experience and track record likely matters to their ability to
generate future returns for their clients, but what looks like past
success may well be just luck.

What is not debatable is that index fund expenses are
extremely low, relative to the expenses of other mutual funds,
and have gotten even lower over time. Conventional equity
index fund expense ratios are six hundredths of a percent; by
contrast, the median equity mutual fund charges more than fif-
teen times the rate that index funds charge. That stark difference makes it even harder for actively managed funds to beat
index funds' results, and for individual investors to do better
by attempting to identify the best active managers out of the
underperforming herd.

Index funds not only charge lower fees, they require less
time and attention from investors. It is vastly simpler for an
individual investor to designate and invest in a reputable low-
cost index fund than it is to invest directly. That would be true
even if a retail investor invested in the same underlying securities as those in an index fund, and even if they could do so at
the same out-of-pocket transaction costs, which they cannot.
That is partly because the components of indexes are constantly changing, as companies merge or otherwise drop out of

34   the market, and new ones are added. An individual investing directly would have to be continually engaged in buying new stocks (along with recordkeeping, tax reporting, and other back office activities) to preserve their exposure to the same diversified investments that a single index fund provides.

Oversight of actively managed funds also takes more time than oversight of index funds. Active strategies must evolve with markets, and key members of good active fund portfolio management teams can retire or leave their roles. Individual investors must devote more attention to monitoring active funds than index funds.

In sum, the value proposition of index funds for individual investors is powerful, even if the basic ideas on which it is built—that stock prices follow a random walk and that paying for financial advice commonly backfires—are counterintuitive or incomplete. Index funds are cheaper, easier to understand, and easier to monitor than other ways to invest.

Growth in Index Fund Investing

As the advantages of index funds became more broadly understood, from 1976 to 2000, index funds steadily but slowly increased their share of stock ownership, as reflected in Table 2.1. Up to the end of the twentieth century, that growth was relatively constrained, culminating in the funds' holding only 2 percent of total US equity market capitalization. In 2000, Morgan Stanley introduced a line of exchange traded funds, which are managed similarly to index funds. That line of business was subsequently sold to Barclays, then to BlackRock, the world's largest asset manager and Vanguard's closest rival in the index fund market. Fidelity, with $4.5 trillion in total assets, was famous for resisting the index fund phenomenon for decades, but it now has more assets in indexed strategies than in actively managed funds, and its total indexed assets make it the fourth of the "Big Four," along with Vanguard, BlackRock, and State Street.

Since 2000, index funds and ETFs have grown more dramatically. Growth has been large both in absolute and relative terms, at a compound annual growth rate of 15 percent over twenty years.

TABLE 2.1.

Growth in Purely Passive Indexed Fund
or ETF Ownership of US Companies, 1990—2020

	(1)	(2)	(3)	(4)	(5)
	US DOMESTIC EQUITY INDEX FUNDS ASSETS $B	(1) AS % OF US EQUITY MARKET CAP	US DOMESTIC EQUITY ETFS ASSETS $B	(3) AS % OF US EQUITY MARKET CAP	PURELY PASSIVE US FUNDS (2) + (4)
1990	n.a.	‹1%	$0	0%	‹1%
2000	$344	2%	$63	‹1%	2%
2010	$701	4%	$476	3%	7%
2020	$3436	8%	$3183	8%	16%

Data sources: Investment Company Institute (for fund assets), World Federation of Exchanges (for market cap).

Passive, indexed US mutual funds and ETFs are now widely understood to hold more than 15 percent of total US equity markets, and 20 percent or more of indexes of large companies, such as the S&P 500 index. When compared to other types of mutual funds, index fund growth has been even sharper. As one report put it, "At year-end 2021, index mutual funds and index ETFs together accounted for 43 percent of assets in long-term funds, up from 21 percent at year-end 2011."

36   In an effort to deflect political suspicion, index fund industry spokespeople sometimes minimize index fund growth with various statistical moves. They report their assets as a share of all global companies or all US companies, for example, which tends to pull down the reported numbers. But for governance and control, it is large cap companies, or the kind that make up the S&P 500, that matter most—to investors, to the economy, and to society. That is where the index funds' holdings are heaviest. Berle and Means identified large public companies as dominant in the American economy a hundred years ago, and that is still the case. It is index fund ownership of those companies that best captures the problem of twelve.

In fact, these data—standard data used in most accounts of the rise of indexed investing—understate the scale and significance of recent growth in indexing. The figures reflected in Table 2.1 represent a lower bound on the share of US equities managed by passive indexed arrangements. They omit assets held by other kinds of institutions, such as pension funds, insurance companies, and nonprofits, which also are often managed in a passive, indexed fashion, often by the same advisor that is advising the other institutions. Also, foreign funds have increased their share of US public equities over the last twenty years. Foreign investors now own approximately 20 percent of all US equities. Much of that ownership is indexed. While precise data on how much are not available, it is fair to assume that a greater portion of foreign ownership of US portfolio companies is truly passive than is the case for domestic. Some of the foreign-owned indexed assets in US public companies are effectively controlled by US index fund advisors.

Finally, a large additional share of assets held in nominally
active funds are in fact practically indexed. That is because active
funds are compared with passive funds for performance. Active
funds commonly minimize management costs by essentially
holding an index and selecting a few companies to over- or
under-weight. This allows them to distinguish themselves from
the index funds, while not attempting to engage in serious analysis of the value of each portfolio company. While Vanguard
largely focuses purely on indexed strategies, the other major
index fund advisors—BlackRock, Fidelity, and State Street—
also manage large actively managed funds, which augment the
governance power they wield by virtue of being large index fund
advisors.

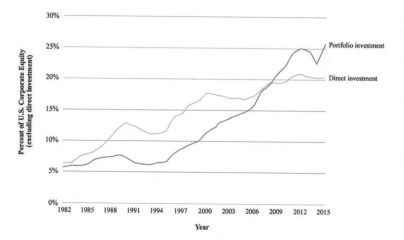

Figure 2.1. Foreign Ownership of US Stocks,
Source: Board of Governors of the Federal Reserve System,
"Financial Accounts of the United States, Tables L230 and L223."

38   All in all, any official data about the financial power of the index funds actually understate the problem of twelve.

Why did index fund ownership take off after 2000? What can the causes of its growth tell us about whether the trend is likely to continue, and for how long?

When indexing was first pioneered, institutions were limited by trust law in the investments they could make. The fiduciary duties of trustees tended to keep money in relatively safe investments. Those duties were relaxed on a state-by-state basis between 1986 and 1997. These legal changes gave trustees both permission and an incentive to invest in line with modern portfolio theory. But that explanation can only go so far. It would explain some of the delay in institutional investment, but not the long, slow rise in indexing by individuals as well as institutions.

Another reason was that the costs associated with keeping track of thousands of fund investors and channeling their investments into hundreds or thousands of public companies declined from 1970 to 2000 due to new technology. The spreadsheet, email, the internet, and other forms of desktop computer technology made their way into the investment world in the 1980s and 1990s. Indexes became easier to produce and distribute.

An additional cause of the migration of capital to index funds was globalization—a lowering of cross-border investment frictions due to the spread of information, along with legal changes reducing barriers to financial trade. Investors know more about their own countries and economies. This makes index fund investing comparatively attractive in a globalizing financial market.

Most important, however, it simply takes a long time for basic but counterintuitive wisdom to penetrate the minds of most ordinary investors. The idea that it makes sense to hire the equivalent of a machine—and a simplistic one at that—rather than an expert human strikes many as hard to believe. How can it make sense to ask one's financial advisor to not think about individual investments?

Employers are increasingly featuring index funds as a default option in 401(k) plans. Pension fund boards are increasingly dedicating a portion of their portfolios to indexed strategies. Discount brokers have eaten into the business of traditional brokers, reducing a source of advice potentially biased toward active management. Once a specific investor realizes the case for indexing, or once an institutional switch of this kind has been made, inertia and the absence of a compelling counter-narrative to bring them back to active management creates the conditions for the steady spread of indexing.

In sum, the main forces leading to the slow but sustained rise of indexed investing are likely to persist into the future. Slow receptivity by retail investors to the idea that they cannot outguess the market themselves, or find investment managers who can, will continue to provide a path for steady growth in indexing. Few active managers will be able to convincingly make the case that they can do better than the market, net of fees, for most index fund investors.

The bottom line is that index funds now own more than 20 percent of large US public companies. If current growth rates continued indefinitely, the entire US market would be held by such funds by 2035. Growth will not be infinite—an equilibrium will eventually be reached, since it gets easier for active

40   funds to outperform index funds as the assets being actively managed fall. But even if the trend flattens, the majority of many public companies will soon be owned by index funds.

Economies of Scale

More important than the sheer growth in indexing is the impact of indexing on concentration. As with capital investment generally, index funds enjoy economies of scale—more so than other types of funds. Indexing is by definition not a high value-added service, nor one on which different investment managers can hope to distinguish themselves. Indexing eschews efforts to beat the market. Index funds do not suffer as they grow, because it is not much harder to match the market at larger scales—all growth requires is to find more shares of stock to buy at current market prices.

By contrast, portfolio managers who do attempt to beat the market find it increasingly more difficult as they deploy ever larger amounts of capital. Brand—built on reliability and low costs—is what matters for index funds, and the value of brand tends to grow, not shrink, with scale.

As a result of economies of scale, index funds and exchange traded funds have increasingly exhibited growth that outstrips their nearest active fund competitors. This is true even in securities such as bonds, where none of Vanguard's index funds were among the top ten in 2000; Vanguard's index fund is now the largest bond fund in the world. Concentration has been even stronger in stocks, where Vanguard's market share has grown at a faster pace. So, too, for the small number of other major index fund providers.

Because of economies of scale and the lack of meaningful   41
margins for differentiation, it is difficult for newcomers to break
into the market. This is in contrast to actively managed funds,
which exhibit continual new entry and turnover. More than 44
percent of assets in US-domiciled equity funds were managed
passively in 2018, up from 19 percent in 2009.

In short, the rise of indexing has increased ownership concentration overall. When actively managed funds dominated
the mutual fund market, their assets were spread among hundreds of advisors. Now that index funds have taken over the
mutual fund market, the number of sizable index funds is tiny.
The result is concentration of ownership in the hands of a very
small number of index fund providers.

The Big Three—Vanguard, State Street, and BlackRock—
now control more than 20 percent of the votes of the S&P
500—a much greater share of US public companies than any
three single investors have ever previously held. And their
stakes continue to rise. In 2017, Vanguard owned 7 percent of
IBM, and each of BlackRock and State Street owned 6 percent,
adding up to 19 percent. By the end of 2018, the Big Three owned
21 percent. The same three fund complexes controlled more
than 20 percent of ConocoPhillips. As noted above, Fidelity is
now also predominantly an index fund advisor—and, when
added to Vanguard, BlackRock, and State Street in a Big Four,
the ownership level rises to 25 percent of the S&P 500 in 2022.

More generally, fund concentration has grown. Almost a
third of the public companies in the S&P 500 have four or fewer
shareholders holding an aggregate of 20 percent or more of their
stock—growth in concentration that is largely attributable to

42 the growth of indexing. In 2005, the top five fund families controlled 35 percent of all regulated fund assets. In 2022, that share had grown to 54 percent. The Big Four own more than 60 percent of the large—5 percent or more of ownership—blocks of stock in the S&P 500.

What's more, these percentages actually understate the ability of the Big Three to affect shareholder votes. Generally, a significant fraction of shareholders does not vote, even if in contested battles, even if held by other types of institutions. As a result, 20 percent ownership actually represents nearly 30 percent of the likely votes in contested elections. That share of the vote will generally be pivotal. Add another few funds, and the votes of other investors that follow the advice of proxy advisory firms such as ISS and Glass Lewis, and the collective vote of the group of indexed investors will almost always include the median vote in such fights.

This is the problem of twelve created by index funds. We no longer live in a Berle-and-Means world. We are rapidly moving into a world in which the bulk of the equity capital of large companies will be owned by a small number of institutions, for the indefinite future. Those institutions, in turn, are controlled by a small number of individuals. For any given company, the ownership rights—most importantly, the right to vote in an election of directors—will be controlled by a small number of individuals working for those institutions. It is not an exaggeration to say that even if this mega-trend begins to taper off, the majority of the thousand largest US companies could be controlled by a dozen or fewer people over the next ten to twenty years.

How do index funds create the problem of twelve, while coexisting with managerialism?

Let us return to corporate governance, to explore how index funds use their assets and to better understand the precise contours of the problem of twelve. A key point is that index funds do not literally control every public company's operations in anything like a full sense. They are careful to not take actions that would lead anyone to claim successfully that they "control" any given public company in a legal sense; instead, they exploit the legal gap between "control" and "influence." That influence is powerful, but constrained. As a result, even as they have generated massive economic benefits for their own investors, they have also stimulated criticism, from a governance perspective, along three lines—for having too much control, for using that control to harm consumers, and for being too deferential to managers.

In a political sense, index funds may present the worst of two worlds—concentration and the risk of too much power, on the one hand, but actual passivity and too little governance activity on the other hand. When they use their power to push companies to do something different, they attract critiques based on the problem of twelve. When they decline to use their power, they attract critiques for failing their jobs as stewards of shareholder wealth. Some index fund spokespeople have pointed to the opposing criticisms as evidence that they are, like Goldilocks, getting it just right. But in the real world of politics, having two inconsistent enemies does not always, or even often, lead to popular support. Indeed, their failure to push a shareholder-wealth agenda aggressively reduces the legitimacy of index funds, even as they are also critiqued for having too much power.

By virtue of owning stock in public companies, index funds obtain theoretical power to engage in governance—voting,

44   monitoring, and engagement. In fact, their legal obligations encourage some (arguably minimal) governance efforts, such as voting. Index fund advisors may also engage in some governance activity for public relations reasons. Governance activity can attract media attention, which can help funds gather more assets in a cost-effective way. (Some argue this was the true motivating factor behind Engine No. 1's activist campaign at ExxonMobil.) But as long as index funds remained a small part of the overall market—that is, up through 2000—they by definition would only own a small part of any one company, and so would have small effects on governance.

As with the dispersed individual investors on behalf of whom they invested, index funds had no rational incentive to engage in much governance activity. Any benefits would be shared with other owners of the portfolio company, but the costs would be borne by the fund and its investors. Few examples of governance activities by a 0.1 percent shareholder can be found that have quantifiable and material benefits for the investor. That is true of both active and passive investors, individuals and institutions alike.

When indexing was starting out, its governance role was not distinct from that of other investors in US public companies. But once index funds had gathered more than 10 percent, and now more than 20 percent, of the shares of all large public companies, their governance potential became much more serious. This is both because of their scale, and because of their relative concentration. A thousand individual shareholders who each owned 0.01 percent of a public company's shares would in theory have the same voting clout as a single fund owning 10 percent. But in real life, the fund has vastly more clout than

individual investors. It is the economies of scale associated   45
peculiarly with index funds that drive concentration, and with
it, governance power.

It enhances index funds' power that they regularly work
with hedge funds, other kinds of institutional shareholders
(particularly pension funds), and governance professionals to
collectively pressure public company managers to act in various
ways. In this division of labor, index funds have real and
increasing influence. This influence takes several forms: policy
influence, influencing and supporting governance activists,
engagements, and, perhaps most importantly, contests for the
overall control of a company.

Index fund advisors formulate and publish policies regarding
various kinds of decisions that the boards and managers of their
portfolio companies must make. These policies are general, not
specific to any one public company. Examples include whether
a company should have staggered terms for board members,
whether its CEO should be paid based on total shareholder
return or on some other metric, and whether the company
should disclose its political activities.

As translated into actual votes at specific companies, the
funds' policy positions inevitably reflect their views about the
management, performance, and strategy of those companies,
even though shareholders do not directly vote on such choices.
Because their actual votes, and often their views, are public,
fund advisors can obtain strong signals about other fund advisors' views on management, performance, and strategy. No
explicit collusion is required to send highly aligned signals
about what they want to each other and to the management of
portfolio companies. Rational managers anticipate goals and

46   preferences of index fund providers, and then enact them, to some extent, without the need for explicit, public directives or exercises of power.

Influencing and Supporting Governance Activists

In addition to having direct policy influence, index fund advisors have increased the power of the network of what are sometimes derogatorily called "governistas" or the "governance machine"—a community of corporate governance activists ranging from academics to public pension fund managers and staff to individual gadflies to the staffs of proxy advisory firms such as ISS and Glass Lewis. As part of this process, index funds meet with other major institutional shareholder representatives, sometimes in events at the author's home institution (Harvard Law School). In these meetings, the participants are careful to confine their discussions to policies and not to specific companies. Still, they collectively form and share views on how these issues should be approached overall, with clear implications for how they will be considered in specific instances. Those views and discussions are part of the way the index fund advisors form policies, which can be tailored to specific circumstances. Through this process, they achieve significant coordination over many if not all topics on which shareholders routinely vote.

As a result, an announcement by a major index fund advisor that it does, or does not, support a given governance position gives greater clout to those who tee up, debate, and form investment community opinion around those issues. For example, even before the ExxonMobil / Engine No. 1 proxy fight, it was BlackRock that pushed Exxon into disclosing the long-term portfolio impacts of global climate change policies. When BlackRock announced its support for a shareholder proposal calling for such disclosure, its announcement did more than just reflect BlackRock's intended vote. It triggered a wave of media coverage, and influenced other institutions and governance professionals to consider similar environmental disclosures more mainstream and acceptable than had previously been the case. BlackRock's announcement preceded a vote in favor of the shareholder proposal by Vanguard, which, media reports noted, had typically lagged environmentally friendly trends in shareholder voting as compared to other large investors in the prior period. This Exxon vote in 2017 led more companies to take action in 2018 in order to avoid losing shareholder votes on the topic, and that likely was a partial reason that Engine No. 1 chose to launch its own campaign when and where it did.

Another channel of influence is through what institutional shareholders call engagements. Their staffs meet—sometimes in person, more often by phone, sometimes just through letters sent by mail or email—with representatives of their portfolio companies. Through these meetings, institutional shareholders try to influence management, by informing them of their policies, their approach to new issues, and their perceptions of management and how it is responding to corporate challenges. These engagements can last a few minutes, or a few hours.

BlackRock's 2019 governance report notes that from July 2018 to July 2019 it "participated in over 2,000 engagements with nearly 1,500 companies," including "multiple meetings" with 375 companies. That level of engagement is a substantial increase from 2017, when BlackRock reported roughly 1,300

48 engagements. State Street reported 1,533 engagements for the same period. Vanguard reported 868, up from 443 in 2014. On specific issues, State Street reported it had engaged with 1,350 companies on board gender diversity, and noted that 43 percent of those companies had "responded to our call by either adding a female director or committing to do so."

Even if the out-of-pocket cost of an engagement (such as a letter) is quite low, the impact of the information provided during the engagement has important effects on portfolio companies, as amplified through the managers of those companies. That is because the engagements provide important signals to managers as to how the investors will behave should votes come up, on issues, or on other matters, including control contests, activist campaigns, or mergers. The prospect of such events—and the power of index fund advisors in those events—provides a powerful incentive to company managers to respond to the wishes of the index funds.

It is this last channel of influence—control contests, activist campaigns, and mergers—where the index funds have their greatest potential for influence. When management proposes a merger requiring a shareholder vote, or when another shareholder—often a hedge fund—proposes a sale, seeks to install individuals on the board, or starts a full-blown proxy contest for control of the company—an index fund's influence grows significantly. As with ordinary shareholder proposals, index fund positions in a disputed merger vote or control contest are typically pivotal if the top index funds take similar positions.

BlackRock reported having voted for 31 percent of dissident proposals in the year ended July 2019, up from 19 percent in 2017. Vanguard reported having participated in over 7,500 merger votes in each of 2018 and 2019, voting no on more than 600 mergers in those two years. While that number is a relatively small fraction of the total number of merger votes, it is large in absolute terms, and large enough to create a meaningful deterrent for managers who are planning a merger proposal, as the costs to both companies and managers of a failed merger vote are significant. State Street reported that 6 percent of their engagements concerned proxy contests, mergers, and acquisitions in the year ended July 2019.

It is true that the direct component of this influence is contingent. For an index fund to exercise actual power through this channel, some other actor has to do something first: an active hedge fund or other activist shareholder needs to propose a resolution or to contest board seats, as in the ExxonMobil fight, or the management of a public company must propose a merger or other event requiring a vote. Nonetheless, managers know these events happen with regularity, and know that index funds will be pivotal to their outcomes.

Specifically, when an index fund engages with a public company, the company's CEO knows there is a meaningful chance that a contest or an activist campaign or a merger will occur before that CEO's tenure is over. CEOs listen with a keen ear in such moments. They know that when shareholders vote, index funds are watching whether the companies do what the shareholders want. Reputations and relationships built in engagements influence future votes.

The bottom line of this review of how index fund advisors use their power to control public companies is neither that they exercise pure control nor that they are passive, in the manner of investors in Berle and Means—style companies in the twentieth

50   century. Rather than blindly choosing stocks in their index and then ignoring them, index fund managers have, and are increasingly using, multiple channels to influence public companies of all sizes and kinds. Their views on governance issues, their opinions of CEOs, their desires for change at particular companies, their response to and evaluations of proposals from hedge fund activists—all of these matter intensely to the way the core institutions in the US economy are operating.

When a large company's performance lags, it is at risk of being targeted by a hedge fund activist. When that occurs, the attitude of the index funds toward that company's management and strategy will determine whether the index funds will support, oppose, or be neutral regarding the hedge fund's proposals. In decisions both ordinary and extraordinary, ranging from cost-cutting to technology investments, M&A transactions to expenditures on corporate compliance, the index funds' perceived pressure on the board will matter.

Those decisions then ripple through the functioning of the economy and society more broadly. Pressure to increase shareholder returns can lead to layoffs. The mere threat of an activist supported by index funds can reduce investment. Reduced budgets for compliance increase the risk of bribery, mass torts, fraud, or antitrust violations. Index fund managers are in a position to increase or decrease the incidence and severity of externalities (e.g., climate change) and rent-seeking (e.g., political corruption). A small number of unelected agents, operating largely behind closed doors, are increasingly important to the lives of millions of people who barely know of their existence, much less their identity or inclinations.

The Rise of
Private Equity

Private equity funds, such as Apollo, Blackstone, Carlyle, and KKR, are doing as much if not more than index funds to erode the legitimacy and accountability of American capitalism, not by controlling public companies, but by taking them over entirely, and removing them from the SEC's disclosure regime. Private equity funds are creating their own problem of twelve.

Private equity firms have moved beyond the buy-strip-sell model of the 1970s and 1980s to become a permanent, parallel capital universe. They now trade businesses among themselves, and have gathered assets at a rate that outstrips growth by public companies and the economy. While index funds are coming to dominate Berle and Means–style companies, private equity funds are shifting increasing amounts of wealth out of those companies altogether, into a separate system of ownership and control. According to reports prepared for the private equity trade group, the US private equity sector employed 11.7 million people in 2020—one in nine private sector workers.

52   Private equity is in part a long-term strategy of regulatory avoidance. Private equity funds are intentionally structured so as not to trigger disclosure laws. The private equity industry helped shape those laws, with lobbying and political influence. Once a private equity fund acquires control of a business, the business goes "dark." The results are less known to researchers and private equity professionals, much less to the public. General assessments of private equity are necessarily tentative. Yet we know enough about private equity to identify another problem of twelve in the making.

One of private equity's signal tricks is to popularize the misleading phrase "private equity." The word "private" in "private equity" connotes the opposite of "public"—a single or small group of owners, perhaps a founding entrepreneur. The label seeks to drape private equity with the legitimacy of private property that public companies lost as their ownership dispersed.

Yet private equity funds do not raise capital from one individual or a small group, and they rarely partner with founders. Rather, they raise capital derived from thousands or even millions of individuals, just as do public companies. The trick is that they do so through other financial institutions, such as pension funds. This allows them to rely on legal fictions to count their owners differently than public companies do. Very little about "private equity" is private in the traditional sense of "private property," as Berle and Means used the phrase.

The Basics of Private Equity

Private equity funds are created by financial advisory firms. Those firms, along with their individual managers, typically invest 1 percent of their own money in a private equity fund's

total capital. As shown in Figure 3.1, the rest of a private equity 53
fund's capital is raised primarily from institutions, such as pension funds. Private equity funds use this capital to invest in operating businesses, just as index funds do.

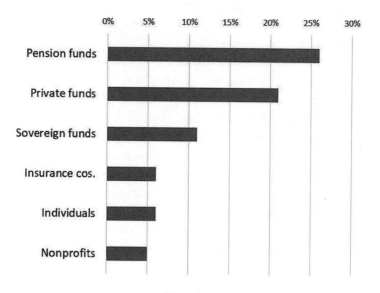

Figure 3.1

Index funds, however, buy stock in small amounts at a time, which in aggregate has grown enormously. Private equity funds usually buy all of the stock of a company, taking it over completely. In the seventies and eighties, these acquisitions were called buyouts. Funds borrowed money, a form of financial leverage, giving them greater buying power, so their deals were called "leveraged buyouts," and the entire industry was known as the LBO industry. That activity persists—most private equity

54 deals are debt-fueled purchases of entire companies. Most private equity assets remain in buyout funds.

Another difference between private equity and index funds is that the latter are heavily regulated. Private equity funds, by contrast, are exempt from this kind of regulation, and private equity advisors are regulated only under the light-touch Investment Advisers Act. Unlike index funds, private equity firms, like venture capital and hedge funds, are permitted to charge potentially lucrative incentive fees. Typically, private equity firms get a 2 percent management fee plus 20 percent of profits. They have a large upside for good outcomes, and even some upside for bad outcomes. Such asymmetric fees—"heads I win, tails you lose"—are illegal for index funds.

Private equity funds' relationships with their own investors also differ from index funds. While index funds provide daily liquidity by redeeming and selling shares, private equity funds collect capital commitments, and once invested in a business, do not allow their investors to exit for many years. Instead, each fund typically has a termination date—effectively a preset commitment to liquidate, seven to twelve years after formation.

As a result, private equity funds plan to exit each business they buy, to generate cash for their investors. They are not truly "flippers"—they rarely buy and sell companies rapidly. However, they are also not long-term investors—their median holding period for a company is six years. At first, private equity exits were initial public offerings. Over time, other exits became more common: sales to public companies; sales to other private equity funds (secondary buyouts); and most recently, sales to new funds managed by the same private equity firm (continuation buyouts).

Private equity firms provide operational and strategic advice to companies they acquire, reshaping operations and even strategy. Because they use debt, they maintain relationships with banks, insurance companies, hedge funds, and other lenders (including other private equity funds). The debt they incur, plus their planned exits, lead private equity firms to try to increase a company's cash flow rapidly. They cut costs, often by laying off employees, cut capital investments, and try to expand profit margins and sales by refining product mixes and marketing strategies.

A private equity firm typically operates at the hub of a wheel, with many private equity funds. Different funds are at the ends of the spokes, in different stages: some in formation, some on the hunt for deals, some exiting prior acquisitions, and some winding up. A private equity complex, as they are called, is in fact complex. In all, private equity is a stylized image of Joseph Schumpeter's "gale of creative destruction" as the "essential fact" of capitalism, characterized chiefly by constant churn—fundraising, dealmaking, and change management as a business.

Today, more than a third of total corporate equity in the US is managed outside of public companies, with the fastest growth in businesses owned by private equity funds. US-based private equity firms have diversified globally, and gone into other financial businesses. They now sponsor or affiliate with hedge funds, broker-dealers, and venture capital funds. Private equity firms now sponsor funds that focus not on traditional buyouts but on real estate and credit.

Private equity's share of the economy continues to grow. Private equity funds were on course to raise more than $1

56   trillion of new capital in 2022. Total assets under management
by private equity funds passed $12 trillion, an all-time record.
Private equity in 2020 managed assets that were 18 percent of
total corporate equity, as measured by the Federal Reserve, compared to 4 percent in 2000. Private equity's assets under management from 2000 to 2020 experienced an astonishingly high
compound annual growth rate of 15 percent, vastly outstripping
the economy overall, which grew at a compound rate of 3.6
percent.

The forerunners of modern private equity funds, instead of
investing in start-ups as venture capital firms do, sought existing
businesses in mature industries and bought them whole. Often
targeting family-owned firms transitioning from the founding
to a second generation, the nascent private equity industry
began to use debt as a key piece of its playbook. Three former
Bear Stearns bankers formed Kohlberg Kravis Roberts in 1976.

As their ambitions grew, KKR and other funds began to
target existing public companies, many of which were performing poorly in the challenging economy of the 1970s. These
deals turned companies from public to private, in the sense that
they were, legally, owned by a single formal owner, the buyout
fund, and no longer had shares trading on a stock exchange.
Post-buyout companies no longer had to comply with SEC disclosure rules. Many saw this consequence of (and motivation
for) buyouts as pernicious, by reducing the ability of the public
generally to understand and trust capitalism.

Going private raises questions about finance. Why would a
concentrated fund pay more for a business than dispersed and
diversified investors? Going private also involved conflicts of
interest. A buyout fund will often ask current managers of a

public company to invest in the buyout—putting the managers on both sides of the deal. Managers (and the fund) would earn more if the deal price were low. Yet as fiduciaries, managers were supposed to protect shareholders by demanding a deal price that was high.

More fundamentally, why should managers profit from post-buyout improvements when pre-buyout shareholders would not? Many believed such buyouts could only make sense if managers were either deliberately underperforming pre-buyout, bringing the price down, or leaking inside information to attract a buyout. When prominent companies are acquired by managers at historically low prices, and taken public again not much later, at a much higher price, going private creates perceptions of abuse, both of information and position. These clouds hang over the industry to this day.

Some legal reforms in the late seventies imposed a stricter review standard on management buyouts. Nonetheless, going private continued, helping contribute to the takeover boom of the 1980s. Indeed, the leverage in leveraged buyouts moved from the margins to the center of corporate finance in the 1980s. The most famous financier of that era, Michael Milken— legendarily wearing a coal-miner's headlamp to read public company annual reports as he commuted from suburban New Jersey to arrive at 4:30 a.m. on Wall Street as a young trader— came to believe one class of securities, in particular, were underpriced: junk bonds.

Junk bonds were debt securities too risky to be investment grade. Those safer bonds were more predictable than stocks, and so were attractive to risk-averse, cautious, or liquidity-demanding investors. Historically, junk bonds were issued by "fallen angels"—companies that had stumbled, leaving debt in danger of default. Milken concluded they had attracted too much stigma, and were, when part of a diversified portfolio, cheap. Buying them would produce above-market returns, even adjusted for risk.

Once retold by enough salesmen, this story allowed junk bonds to take off. Importantly, too, even the riskiest bonds at the time generated tax-deductible interest payments. With corporate tax rates high, this provided, in effect, a public tax-payer subsidy for the investment product, giving a lift to the rise in leveraged buyouts.

The scale of leveraged buyouts soared, bringing into their range companies of increasing size and prominence. By 1989, some of the world's largest companies were buyout targets.

Buyouts and buyout funds grew in number as well as assets. Bain Capital was founded in 1984, Blackstone in 1985, and Carlyle in 1987. What had been a minor part of finance became a distinct and lucrative profession. Henry Kravis became a household name (at least in households talking about Wall Street). HBO produced *Barbarians at the Gate*.

Buyouts intertwined with two other features of the 1980s: hostile takeovers and insider trading. Stimulated by globalization and the challenging economy of the 1970s, buyout funds competed with and were given new roles by the corporate raiders of the 1980s. Swashbucklers like Texas oilman T. Boone Pickens denounced the managers of the entire oil and gas industry as incompetent sloths, and extracted greenmail with threats of hostile takeover bids. Buyers dramatically restructured their targets, forcing divestitures, downsizing, or liquidation. Layoffs and plant closures swept America: one in five blue-collar workers lost their jobs from 1981 through 1983. Prominent economists such as Larry Summers and Andrei Shleifer analyzed these takeovers of the 1980s as a "breach of trust" with workers and communities.

As buyouts crested, cheerleaders like Harvard Business School's Michael Jensen predicted that public companies were the next dodo, soon to be extinct. Instead, leveraged buyouts overshot and succumbed to scandal. In 1986, Drexel Burnham hit its peak earnings of $545.5 million, the most ever by a Wall Street firm. Dennis Levine, a Drexel banker, also plead guilty to four felonies that year, and the SEC opened an investigation, eventually suing Drexel for insider trading, manipulation, and fraud.

After uncovering secret, likely illegal trades by Milken, Drexel plead guilty and agreed to a $650 million penalty, then the largest fine ever under the securities laws. The junk bond market shut down. Over the next year, junk bond defaults doubled, and Drexel went bankrupt, as did Macy's and Trans World Airlines. Hundreds of banks and S&Ls failed, Milken went to prison, and the economy entered a recession.

Some wondered if buyouts would recover. No high-profile buyouts occurred for years, although new funds did get created (Apollo in 1990 and Texas Pacific Group in 1992). Few anticipated that buyout firms would begin a dramatic expansion that would carry on for the next quarter century. Even fewer expected a key to this era of expansion would lie in politics.

The Liquidation of Legal Constraints on Private Funds and the (Re)birth of "Private Equity"

As large as buyouts got in the 1980s, the industry remained a small subsector of finance. Firms focused on buyouts remained

60   tiny relative to banks and insurance companies. Kohlberg Kravis Roberts had sixty employees in 1989, when Citibank employed 50,000 and Merrill Lynch 44,000. KKR today has thousands of employees, and hundreds of professionals. What accounts for the rebirth and transformation of the industry from the mid-1990s?

Any answer has to include politics, PR, lobbying, and deregulation. Private equity funds throughout their history have benefited from lobbying by the National Venture Capital Association, formed in 1973 by leading venture capital firms. By dressing up their goals as deregulatory, venture capital and private equity lobbying efforts have achieved respectability among a large segment of the public. Many of the policy changes they pursue have classic hallmarks of rent-seeking and interest group protection. They rarely achieve exclusively deregulatory ends. Much taxpayer-subsidized venture capital investment generates profits for large financial institutions and public companies. Yet the public relations value of associating venture capital and private equity with small business endures as a lobbying trope.

Lobbying bore fruit throughout the Carter/Reagan era of deregulation. In 1978, the SEC allowed entrepreneurs to raise up to $500,000 free of regulation—a genuine small business reform. Pressed by lobbies, however, Congress broadened the exemption in 1980, and in response, in 1982, the SEC created a big new set of loopholes in securities law, known as Reg D, which helped pave the way for massive modern private equity firms.

Reg D permits unlimited amounts of capital raising by any business from an unlimited number of moderately wealthy accredited investors. Genuinely small businesses utilize Reg D. But over time, so did many businesses that could in no way be called small, including the 2010s herd of technology "unicorns" (non-SEC-registered companies valued at $1 billion or more), such as Bolt, Reddit, and Grammarly, each of which has more than five hundred employees.

The venture capital and private equity industries achieved gains on other lobbying fronts as well.

- In 1978, the Department of Labor relaxed its "prudent man" rule, permitting pension funds to make riskier investments, including in venture capital and buyout funds.
- In 1981, Congress created a research and development tax credit, which is still on the books. That credit subsidizes such supposedly cutting-edge research as new menu items for restaurants and smartphone apps that assess social media mentions.
- In 1982, Congress mandated federal agencies to set aside funding for businesses with fewer than five hundred employees, in amounts that increased by 1997 to $1.1 billion per year. Nominally for any small business, more than 40 percent of the awards flow to venture capital–dominated states (California and Massachusetts), with individual companies often receiving multiple awards.

The biggest payoff from the political partnership between the venture capital and private equity lobbies (later joined by hedge funds) came in 1996, in a shift still underappreciated by many observers of the US capital markets. The lobbying effort took aim at one of the biggest legal constraints on private equity funds, the Investment Company Act of 1940. That law restricts leverage, limits incentive compensation, and imposes

62   transparency on regulated funds. All those goals conflict with
the private equity firm business model.

The passage of the National Securities Markets Improvement Act of 1996 is an exemplar of Bill Clinton's initiatives that
benefited financial interests at the expense of the public. The
act let funds raise unlimited capital from unlimited numbers of
institutions or individuals with $5 million in investments.
Previously, private funds were limited to a hundred investors.
From 1996 on, private equity funds (and venture capital and
hedge funds) could raise capital from hundreds or even thousands of institutions. With most of their capital now invested
through institutions, private equity funds could stay dark
without any regulatory limit on their scale.

The result has been that private equity funds have scaled
up dramatically. Not coincidentally, the 1996 act preceded a
long drop-off in initial public offerings by US companies. From
1996 on, companies increasingly chose to delay or avoid altogether public listings and the transparency of public disclosures and SEC oversight. Only in 2021, amid unusually if briefly
favorable market conditions, did IPOs again experience a significant increase.

The Brilliant, Deceptive Rebranding of Buyout Funds as "Private Equity" Funds

Less tangible but also important to the resurgence of buyout
funds was a rebranding exercise. Well aware that the borrow-
buy-layoff-or-go-bust model of large leveraged buyouts had
been politically controversial from the outset, and had stumbled badly in 1989, buyout firms searched for a new label, ultimately settling on private equity.

That phrase had long been used primarily to refer to the owners of any company not registered with the SEC. It included venture capital–backed and founder- or family-owned companies. In a concerted and ultimately successful effort, buyout firms of the 1980s managed to convince the world to speak as if the leveraged buyout industry had ceased to exist. Even industry critics now talk about it with a less politically fraught phrase, private equity.

The rebranding is evident in how firms were covered in business news from 1980 to 2000. In the mid-1980s, KKR proudly billed itself as a "buyout specialist." After the bust in 1989, it pivoted to distressed investing, but continued to be identified as a buyout firm. But it then began increasingly to pursue what it billed "leveraged buildups"—using portfolio companies and debt to fund many smaller acquisitions in the same industries. By 1994, for example, KKR's K-III fund had spent $461 million to buy two hundred different publications. In 1995, an analyst noted unnamed observers arguing that such buildups showed that the "buyout business has evolved into a private equity finance business." By 1996, as KKR raised the second-largest fund in history, it was described in the *Financial Times* as an investment firm with performance "nearly on par with . . . other private equity funds." While memories of KKR's R. J. Reynolds leveraged buyout may never die entirely, KKR is now most frequently labeled simply as a private equity firm. In its 390-page 2021 annual report, it uses the word "buyout" precisely once (in reference to management buyouts), and the phrase "private equity" 193 times.

One need not believe the public ever forgot buyouts were happening to admire the bravura of the rebranding. Harvard faculty helped, introducing a course in the 1993–1994 academic year labeled as "Venture Capital and Private Equity." Perhaps unwittingly, so did the Federal Reserve Board, in a 1996 study based on industry interviews. That study lumped venture capital with buyout funds, which it called "Non-Venture Private Equity."

By adopting new nomenclature, private equity firms shed the negative connotations of leveraged buyouts: excessive debt, layoffs, and bankruptcy. But the rebranding achieved a subtler and also important (and deceptive) goal: to hide the nature of their economic ownership of companies they controlled. Private connotes the opposite of public. This implies a small number of investors have interests in companies owned by private equity funds—otherwise, they would have to register with the SEC. Legally and formally, in fact, a portfolio company of a private equity fund has one shareholder—the fund itself. The private equity brand implies privacy, private property, and private initiative of a single owner firm—all attributes that Berle and Means argued large public companies had lost in the early twentieth century, as ownership dispersed among thousands of investors.

What is deceptive about the private equity brand is the nature of private equity funds' own investors. Private equity funds do not raise much capital from a few wealthy individuals, as once was the case. They raise most of their money from institutions. Each institution itself raises capital from (or holds it on behalf of) hundreds or thousands of people. As a result, the economic beneficiaries of one private equity fund number in the thousands. Private equity funds and firms in no way eliminate the issues Berle and Means raised in 1932. The capital put at risk by private equity firm owners is just as much "other people's money" as it is when invested in public companies. Businesses

owned by the private equity industry no more deserve the con-   65
notations of "private" than General Motors or Exxon do. Indeed,
private equity firms have been growing faster than public companies, and concentrating in a way that public companies are
not and have never been concentrated.

The Dramatic Expansion of "Private Equity" from 1995 to Today

With the laws relaxed, the 1990–91 recession fading in memory,
and, a better brand in place, private equity funds grew steadily
from a low point in the early 1990s. By 2000, the earliest year
for which consistent if incomplete and unverified data are
available, private equity funds had roughly $770 billion of global
assets under management. By 2021, buyout funds had amassed
global assets of $12.1 trillion.

Private equity grew four to five times faster than the US
economy as a whole.

It was most notable in a large buyout wave in the mid-2000s.
Among all-cash deals, private equity deals represented more
than a quarter of all merger and acquisition activity from 2006
to 2010. This compares to less than a tenth during the 1980s. As
the US economy approached the financial crisis of 2007–08,
private equity firms wrote ever-larger checks to buy ever-larger
companies. Mega-buyouts in 2007 alone included TXU Energy
(KKR, $32 billion), First Data (KKR, $26 billion), Alltel (Atlantis,
$25 billion), and Hilton Worldwide (Blackstone, $20 billion).
The TXU buyout remains the largest of all time, outstripping
even KKR's more famous 1989 buyout of R. J. Reynolds.

Private equity generates more profits for Wall Street than
any other industry. In the mid-2000s, bank fees from private

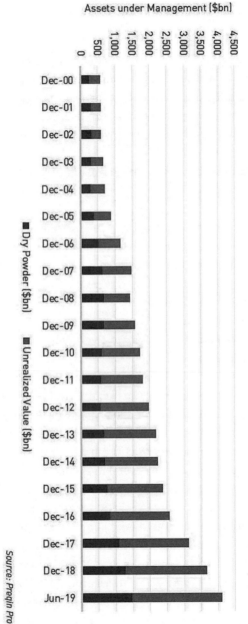

Figure 3.2: Preqin chart showing rise in AUM from 2000 to 2021

Source: Preqin Pro

equity outstripped the fees from traditional corporate clients.
Partly this massive flow of money follows from the basic buyout business model: buying to sell. Private equity funds buy
and sell companies every five to ten years. They do more deals
more frequently than public companies, even companies active
in mergers and acquisitions. Private equity firms also generate
fees to banks because of their consistent heavy use of new loan
syndications.

The 2007–08 financial crisis—with high-profile private
equity deal failures and bankruptcies—might have been expected
to dampen these trends. It did not. Since the crisis, as Wall
Street has recovered, private equity firms remain central to
ongoing deal activity. From 2005 to 2010, General Electric and
General Motors were the only public company clients among
the top ten payers of investment bank fees. In 2010, the $10 bil-
lion in fees paid by private equity comprised 14 percent of total
investment bank revenues of $69 billion. Private equity is the
core of Wall Street.

Not only has private equity grown, it has grown faster than
either public companies or the overall economy. Harvard
Business School researchers Josh Lerner and Paul Gompers
reported in 1997 that the amount of capital invested in public
companies was forty times bigger than in private equity. Today,
the ratio is twelve times—an increase of 300 percent in private
equity's share. Of the assets controlled by private equity firms,
most remain in buyout funds.

Private equity firms have also leveraged their roles to
increase their share of other types of financial assets. In addition to equity—ownership in companies—they own more
than $3 trillion of debt, real estate, and infrastructure. Public

68   companies remain the dominant form of economic organization in the US, but companies owned by private equity firms are steadily expanding their relative importance. Their growth is particularly strong during periods of high merger activity, and in a subset of industries.

In 2021, private equity firms announced a record $1.2 trillion worth of deals. In 2022, private equity did 25 percent of all mergers and acquisitions, an all-time high. Dealmaking by private equity firms is far less sensitive to macroeconomic and financial fluctuations than deals among and by public companies. Private equity funds exert outsized importance in industries they helped consolidate. In "roll-ups," a single buyer targets an industry, often one dominated by small or midsized companies. The buyer engages in multiple acquisitions, consolidating them into one larger company. Over time, buyers acquire experience in driving down costs and leveraging control and information systems at scale. Such strategies have long been used by public companies.

Private equity firms have increasingly used this strategy, which they sometimes call a "leveraged build-up." Having built up a company this way, they then exit (that is, sell the company) as usual. Relying on their strong relationships in credit markets, private equity firms can raise cheaper capital to execute a roll-up than other buyers.

Industries rolled up by private equity are even more private equity—dominated than the economy overall. Private equity firms focus on mature and stable but geographically dispersed businesses—nursing homes, housing, food service, and personal service businesses. Small-company roll-ups often avoid antitrust scrutiny, due to the size thresholds in antitrust law.

Roll-up buyers can obtain market power within local markets
without being noticed as quickly, or perhaps at all, by the Justice
Department or the Federal Trade Commission.

Concentration Among Private Equity Firms:
A Second Problem of Twelve

Roll-ups are just one way private equity increases concentration
of power over the economy. At first, this observation may seem
puzzling, because there are today many more private equity
complexes than ever before. In 2013, when the SEC began col-
lecting data on private equity firms, 815 were in operation. Today
there are more than twice that number. But while there are more
funds, most private equity funds are (relatively) tiny. The bulk of
the industry's assets are accumulating within the largest private
equity fund complexes, particularly the very top ones. The four
largest private equity complexes—Blackstone, KKR, Carlyle,
and Apollo—report assets totaling $2.7 trillion. By contrast, the
median private equity fund size is a mere $100 million.

As a result, concentration of control over businesses by a
few private equity firms has been increasing over time. Because
private equity firms are increasingly important to the overall
economy, especially in some industries, and because their
assets are flowing to the largest firms, private equity firms, no
less than index fund complexes, represent a new concentration
of wealth and corresponding power. Private equity firms, in
sum, are generating another problem of twelve.

Private equity concentration is less dramatic and evident
than for index funds, but in some ways, it is more threatening,
because of the darkness that is a core feature of private equity, as
well as the close connections between private equity and Wall

70   Street, and the high-powered incentives private equity uses to motivate professionals and reshape businesses. Index funds at least report to the SEC and the public about their holdings; private equity funds are designed to be opaque. Even as the industry has repeatedly invested in efforts to burnish its reputation among the public and elected officials, it continues to resist transparency laws.

Index fund sponsors have also pursued a light touch approach to corporate governance to date, mainly to keep costs low. Private equity firms, by contrast, seek to increase the cash thrown off by companies they buy, and to do so quickly enough to exit at a profit within a few years of a purchase. Private equity firms' cultures vary, but as an industry, private equity is demanding. It is proudly ruthless in how rapidly and powerfully it changes the companies it buys. The firms are more likely to change the ways their companies affect customers, employees, communities, or the environment than companies owned by individuals or families, or mid-twentieth-century public companies.

In addition to becoming more concentrated, private equity funds increasingly cooperate rather than compete. Obviously, funds controlled by a single private equity firm work as allies, not as competitors. KKR in 2021 had nineteen private equity funds in current operation. More important, private equity funds controlled by different advisors commonly join together to buy a single target company, in what are called club deals, and increasingly they sell their portfolio companies not to public companies, or to dispersed investors, but to each other, in what are called secondary buyouts. Finally, old-fashioned oligopolistic collusion has begun to emerge in some industries in which multiple private equity funds own businesses.

In club deals, two or more private equity firms team up to bid for a single target company. Broader cooperation, with three or more private equity firms joining forces, has also grown more common in large deals. In 1990, 7 percent of private equity buyouts involved three or more private equity firms. By 2000, three-firm club deals had risen to 17 percent, and by 2010 they represented over 22 percent of all private equity buyouts. If one examines bids involving just two or more private equity firms, the trend was stronger: as early as 2004, more than 40 percent of US buyouts were club deals.

Club deals can permit collusion—through a form of club etiquette—to keep prices down, particularly in deals to take public companies private. Club deals require close and intimate communication among private equity professionals in particular acquisitions. Over time, such communication provides ideal cover for discussing allocating deals among private equity firms (an antitrust no-no), while creating a false appearance of competition.

One private equity firm might agree to bid low in one deal, allowing another to win at a lower price than if both competed normally. In going-private deals, buyers and targets must announce a deal and seek shareholder approval, at which point other bidders can jump the signed deal. Private equity firms who routinely clubbed could collude to bid only prior to a deal announcement. Then, in the next opportunity, they would trade places. Among private equity firms, this could systematically lower prices and reduce returns to the target companies' shareholders.

In 2007, a class action lawsuit accused seven prominent private equity firms—KKR, Blackstone, TPG, Bain, Goldman

72   Sachs, Silver Lake, and Carlyle—of conspiring to fix prices in eight of the historically large transactions that took place during the private equity deal wave of the 2000s. Pension funds and individuals who had owned shares in target companies argued that the private equity firms had developed an informal quid pro quo system in which they would not bid aggressively on specific deals, particularly after going-private deals were announced.

In September 2006, for example, a club led by Blackstone agreed to buy a semiconductor company called Freescale for $17.6 billion. Instead of counterbidding, Henry Kravis told Blackstone that KKR would be "standing down." Blackstone's president wrote to KKR: "Together we can be unstoppable but in opposition we can cost each other a lot of money. I hope to be in a position to call [to form a club with] you [in] a large exclusive [going private deal] in the next week or 10 days."

KKR's George Roberts replied: "Agreed."

Blackstone soon invited KKR into a new club to buy Clear Channel, the country's number-one owner of radio stations. Similar examples fill a 221-page complaint.

While asserting the lawsuit was without merit, all seven firms settled the dispute as the trial date approached. With deep financial pockets and the best lawyers in the world, the firms explained they were settling a spurious case merely to end the distraction of litigation. The price they were willing to pay to eliminate this distraction? Altogether, plaintiffs were paid $590 million.

Whether collusion continues, or was more widespread than the eight deals in the 2007 lawsuit, remains disputed. One academic study found shareholders receive 40 percent lower

premiums in club deals compared to what they get in sole-
sponsored buyouts. Of course, club bidding might arise for
good economic reasons overall, but also provide a channel for
collusive price-fixing. Club deals for a time became less
common; in 2018, the share of deals involving two or more private equity firms was 20 percent, well below the peak in the
mid-2000s. But the diminishment of club deals is itself a strike
against the arguments used to justify them. If they in fact were a
way for private equity firms to add value, they would have continued, with more attention to avoiding damning emails that
suggested back-scratching and price-fixing.

Another way that private equity firms routinely
communicate—increasingly so—is through what are called secondary buyouts. "Secondary" simply means that one private
equity fund sells a company to another private equity fund. The
business remains within the private equity industry, but its
owners shift. Secondary buyouts emerged in the 1990s, and by
2000–2004, they comprised over 20 percent of the total transaction value in the industry. Since 2018, they have accounted for
half of all private equity exits.

Secondary buyouts pose a puzzle. Private equity advocates
long pointed to the shock treatment they deliver to companies,
in the form of debt, hands-on governance, and higher-powered
incentives, to explain how buyouts add value. But the current
owner of a company in a secondary buyout has already applied
private equity's shock treatment. Unless the first private equity
firm failed to use the private equity playbook, how could a
second private equity owner add value? And if the first private
equity firm failed to use the private equity playbook, why would
the second pay more than the first has already paid?

74   One answer may be that the increase in the number of private equity funds has led them to specialize. Some private equity firms focus on businesses at an earlier stage of their life cycle, others on later stages. Secondary buyouts can represent a handoff by one specialist to another. Alternatively, some private equity firms may specialize in operations, while others focus more on pure financing. An especially poorly run business might be acquired by an operationally focused private equity firm, which improves it but is incapable of squeezing all financial synergies out of its ownership, and so sells it to a larger private equity firm that has better access to cheap capital.

However, secondary buyouts may arise for less admirable reasons. Private equity buyers may be approaching the end of a fund's life. Secondary buyouts may be fast ways to fill out a fund's investment record, generating additional fees. These motives might lead secondary private equity buyers to overpay. Private equity sellers, meanwhile, may provide a quick exit in liquidating a fund at the very end of its life, or to realize profits before a new round of fundraising. Such sellers might be willing to undervalue a business being sold. As with club deals, private equity firms might have informal quid pro quos, sometimes as buyers, sometimes as sellers, to help each other manage fund wind-ups and fundraising.

Also of concern are some broader implications of secondary buyouts. Secondary buyouts are contributing to the permanence of private equity ownership. No longer is private equity ownership transitory—temporarily shielding a company from disclosure laws and public scrutiny, eventually to return it to public status. Instead, large portions of whole industries are disappearing indefinitely into private equity darkness. And

concentration is particularly acute in the secondary sector of
the private equity industry. McKinsey & Co.'s 2022 annual
report on private equity reported that, in such deals, 40 percent
of capital raised in the last five years went to just five firms. As
buyouts increasingly occur between private equity funds, the
firms involved are the largest. They own a disproportionate
share of businesses in such transactions. Secondary buyouts are
a channel for the industry's growing problem of twelve.

Not surprisingly, as private equity firms have increased
their share of the economy, they have been caught up in price-
fixing cartels and other illegalities. In April 2014, the European
Commission found producers of underground and submarine
high voltage power cables, among them a portfolio company
owned by Goldman Sachs's private equity unit, had been operating a cartel. Goldman was fined €37 million. In November
2014, the Netherlands fined a cartel in the flour industry, which
included three private equity firms. In 2022, private equity firm
Lion Capital was dragged into a lawsuit alleging cartel conduct
by the company owning Bumble Bee tuna. No rigorous analysis
yet suggests private equity owners are any worse in this area
than other owners, but as private equity expands, the antitrust
harms its companies cause will likely grow.

From Shock Treatment to Permanent Owners
A final set of developments in the private equity industry over
the past twenty years illustrates how important, durable, and
adaptable the industry is in pursuing not only profit but also
scale and scope.

The essence of private equity is that ownership is by enti-
ties that are not public companies required to be registered with

76   the SEC and subject to general public disclosure requirements. Yet since 2007, nine of the top private equity firms have themselves become public companies. Starting with KKR and Blackstone, followed by Carlyle, Apollo, Oaktree, Ares, and most recently TPG, major buyout firms have all dispersed their ownership, obtaining the liquidity that stock exchange listing brings, and subjecting themselves to SEC registration and disclosure. Two other top private equity fund sponsors—Goldman and Brookfield—pursue diversified businesses and have long been public companies, and both of their private equity arms focus on real estate and non-US assets. Only Ardian, of the major private equity companies, remains private.

This seems puzzling. How can firms operate private equity funds and yet be public companies? Does the public-company status of large private equity firms solve the problem of twelve they create? The short answers to these questions are that private equity firms and private equity funds differ, and no—the problem of twelve remains intact.

It is the private equity firms, not private equity funds or the portfolio companies that private equity funds own, that have gone public. Publicly held private equity firms now report about their advisory operations, the management fees they collect, their costs of fund formation and fundraising, and other aspects of the business of sponsoring and managing private equity funds. But they do not report about operations and activities of their portfolio companies, or details about the funds themselves.

The contrast between private equity firm transparency and private equity fund opacity shows up in numbers. As of this writing, KKR's equity market capitalization—as a public private equity firm—is about $57 billion. That is large. However, KKR reports assets under management in its private equity funds at $195 billion, vastly larger. Those assets, moreover, are leveraged. By having its funds borrow to buy portfolio companies, KKR can roughly double the equity it invests. By relying on other people's money this way, KKR's displacement of transparent public companies in the economy is much bigger than its own market value would suggest.

To see how this matters, note that Blackstone's funds own American Campus Communities, Inc., the largest developer/manager of student housing in the US; PS Business Parks, a large developer of multi-tenant commercial properties; and CoreTrust, a large hospital supply company. Yet investors can find no information about those companies in Blackstone's SEC reports. Blackstone discloses nothing about the rents or vacancy rates in its student housing, about the commercial real estate it is developing, or about its hospitals' supply costs. That is because these businesses are not owned by Blackstone, but by Blackstone funds. Blackstone advises the funds, and gets paid fees by them, but the funds are private.

The public status of private equity firms lets those firms raise more capital to sponsor more private funds. By disclosing a slice of information about the top-level investment management companies, private equity firms increase their ability to own and control businesses about which they need disclose next to nothing to the public. Even their fund investors can get information only of a limited nature. At the same time, the private equity firms demonstrate through their own governance

78 and ownership as public companies that there is nothing particularly socially disadvantageous about public company status.

Public company status and greater fundraising power has also enabled private equity firms to expand their geographic reach. In the eighties, private equity focused on US markets. Since then, private equity has gone global, bringing private equity techniques to Europe and increasingly to Asia, Africa, and South America. Blackstone's latest annual report touts itself as a "global leader" investing on a "global basis" drawing on "global relationships" in the "global economy." At the same time, it provides no geographic information about its portfolio companies.

Another private equity innovation is the use of continuation funds. These are created by a private equity firm to buy companies from its other funds. Similar to secondary buyouts, continuation buyouts keep deals, fees, and control within the same private equity complex.

Continuation funds, conflicts, and recycling are on the rise. Buyouts by continuation funds obviously involve conflicts of interest. The buyer and seller are both controlled by the same private equity firm. Recognizing this, fund investors expect and private equity firms provide third-party valuations as a check on the deals, to try to prevent either fund involved from being disadvantaged.

The SEC has uncovered other potential conflicts during investigations of private equity activities. Examples include expense allocation, deals between private equity firms and portfolio companies owned by their funds, and the expansion of private equity firms into other asset classes. In a February 2015 speech, an SEC official said that nearly all SEC private

equity—related enforcement matters involve conflicts of interest
and disclosures to fund investors about conflicts.

Even if continuation deals are adequately policed, they inarguably demonstrate how the private equity industry has become a separate, permanent governance and capital sector in the US economy. Once a fund in a private equity complex buys a business, it can be sold . . . to another fund in the same complex. Many such funds are devoted to specific assets, including businesses. They permit a private equity firm to repay fund investors while preserving the private non-SEC-registered status of a given company controlled by the firm.

Related to continuation funds is what is called recycling of funds. A given private equity fund may sell an asset to get cash, which in traditional private equity practice would be paid to fund investors. Through recycling, which is permitted by most private equity fund contracts, the private equity firm can retain the cash in its fund and reinvest it in another business. Again, the overall effect is to make more permanent the capital overseen by private equity firms.

A third feature of the contemporary private equity world is another example of clever public relations. Growth capital, growth funds, and growth buyouts are phrases increasingly used to capture what once was called buyout or private equity activity. In their narrowest form, growth buyouts are acquisitions of high-growth businesses, such as (recently) software-as-a-service firms. Because these businesses are far from steady-state mature firms, and are still growing rapidly, they predictably need more capital to sustain growth after the acquisition.

In 2014, for example, Clearlake Capital bought a growing cloud services firm, ConvergeOne, for less than $100 million.

(Clearlake made headlines in 2022 by buying Chelsea FC, the UK football club.) Over three years, Clearlake built up ConvergeOne through multiple acquisitions, funded with $700 million in debt. Having expanded cash flow by 400 percent, ConvergeOne went public, with Clearlake retaining a majority interest. In 2018, Clearlake agreed to sell the entire company to another private equity firm, CVC Capital, for $1.8 billion in a secondary buyout, netting Clearlake a massive 1,000 percent return.

Growth buyouts of this kind reflect the final abandonment of the buyout model from the seventies and eighties. They demonstrate how completely private equity has become a separate, alternative capital universe. Today, venture capital and growth equity combined make up 47 percent of private equity fundraising. Private equity firms now manage the full range of businesses that once exclusively took the form of Berle-and-Means public companies.

Private equity has struggled with its reputation from the get-go. It has been implicated in insider trading, managerial abuse, and excessive debt and risk-taking from its buy-strip-and-flip business model. In the eighties, it was associated with the fictional Gordon Gekko's "greed is good" culture and with such real-life felons as Michael Milken. Private equity was arguably a major cause of the 1989–91 recession, and while it was not a major cause of the 2008 crisis, private equity's push-the-envelope approach to financial risk led to ruin for scores of businesses—even as private equity firms protected themselves with their heads-I-win-tails-you-lose structures. With growth in size, so, too, came growth in misbehavior: collusion in club deals, conflicts of interest in secondary and continuation deals, and SEC enforcement actions about fees and fraud.

But buyout funds have always operated under a more basic
cloud, the mystery of how they make money. How can a financial
buyer add real value to a business? Why can't companies adjust
their finances themselves? This mystery is reinforced by their
lack of disclosure.

Economists Franco Modigliani and Merton Miller earned
Nobel Prizes in part for demonstrating that capital structure—
finance—should not affect the value of a business, except due
to market imperfections. What market imperfections might
explain private equity's ability to earn profits? One conventional answer is tax policy.

Private equity exploits the line-drawing that is inevitable in
any tax system. It does so in two main ways: through debt, which
is taxed more favorably than equity, and through capital investments, returns on which are taxed more favorably than wages or
salaries. Private equity firms generate more profits, relative to
other companies, by engaging in tax arbitrage over these two
definitional lines (debt versus equity and investment versus
employment).

Debt is central to how private equity funds buy companies.
After a buyout, the funds' portfolio companies have more debt
than other companies. Up to a point, debt is taxed more favorably than equity. Interest on debt is deductible, which reduces
income tax, while dividends on equity are not. Private equity
firms are also paid in part in the form of carried interest, the
performance fee that is typically set at 20 percent of profits.
Because this fee is based on growth in the value of an asset (a
business), it is treated for tax purposes as an investment return.
Capital gains on investments are taxed more lightly than ordinary income, and deferred until they are realized in cash. Private

82   equity firms are essentially able to pay themselves (out of fund profits) more cheaply than if they were simply earning advisory fees.

Yet if taxes were the sole explanation for private equity profits, private equity firms would still have a legitimacy deficit. Why should tax law reward risky borrowing? Why should the public pay higher taxes to make up for the smaller tax base private equity creates and the lower rates private equity enjoys, particularly since private equity professionals work with assistants who have higher tax rates?

A second possibility—another market imperfection—is that private equity firms have more information than others. To some extent the skeptical view is right—management buyouts can be a form of institutionalized insider trading and ethical abuse by managers, aided and abetted by private equity. For a CEO to partner with private equity, borrow to buy his own company from the shareholders he was working for, and then take the company public again a short time later, earning profits far beyond ordinary CEO salaries, still strikes observers as abusive.

However, these abuses cannot be the whole private equity story. Most buyouts do not involve management on the buy side, and many businesses bought by private equity funds are sold by single owner-managers, who cannot misappropriate information from themselves. Private equity buyers could not afford to systematically bribe exiting managers with over-inflated payouts as a way of generating deals, and still profit over a short holding period. In any event, no private equity firm is willing—even in private—to admit that insider trading or opportunism explains their success.

A less damning version of the better information explanation is that private equity firms have better access to market information. As a result, even without inside information derived from selling managers, they are better at selecting companies to buy, or at timing their deals. Legally, they are free to use such market information, if it weaves minor facts into a tapestry of material information, or if it is derived from patterns to which the firms have legal access (that is, not through insiders at public companies). For example, one study suggests private equity managers are systematically able to foresee comparable public firms' earnings, and to use that information to sell portfolio companies at industry peaks when they have performance fees to harvest. This information-based explanation is tied to their central role in the capital markets.

To avoid bragging about tax arbitrage or insider trading, private equity backers since the 1980s have told a different story. It is that private equity's basic design produces better management. Through debt, compensation, and governance mechanisms, private equity firms improve the incentives of managers to operate profitably.

Debt helps not because it is cheaper than equity, or even primarily because of its tax advantages. Rather, sharp increases in debt force companies to improve cash flow rapidly to service that debt, or else. Financial risk elicits a Puritan work ethic. To debt's discipline, private equity's 20 percent upside adds incentives to increase value, shared with managers who co-invest. Tight governance—no large, part-time boards sleeping through glib management presentations before an expensive dinner— enables rapid interventions to keep a company steady in difficulties or amid strategic changes. Together, this package provides

84   shock treatment to mature companies that had been rendered inertial or flabby by complacent, under-incentivized managers. Or they add discipline to second-generation owners of once-thriving family business hampered by nepotism.

For buyouts from the 1980s, evidence suggests this story has merit. Many public companies started that decade with little debt, had passive, uninformed boards, and gave few incentives to managers to take risky or difficult actions to improve value. CEOs increased their salaries and bonuses by growing their empires and their revenues at the expense of profits. Many used shareholder funds to buy corporate jets, and one—infamously—took his German shepherd along for a ride. The economic challenges of the seventies and eighties caught many firms flat-footed. Active owners like private equity firms likely did improve value with better governance.

This explanation may continue to hold true for middle-market or family-owned firms. But today's public companies no longer resemble their predecessors. Managers no longer take American hegemony for granted; globalization and its challenges are actively managed every moment of every day in any industry exposed to trade. CEOs are now paid significantly in stock and stock options, and so have strong incentives to increase their companies' share prices. Corporate debt is significantly higher overall than it was in the early 1980s. Boards are smaller, tougher, more skilled, and much more likely to intervene if a company's profits stall. Activist hedge funds emerged in the nineties that constantly monitor and pressure public companies to do precisely the kinds of things private equity funds did in the eighties.

Institutional shareholders began to exert pressure on their   85
own in the eighties, and they no longer routinely approve
management-proposed empire-building deals. As a result,
public companies frequently engage in restructurings, divestitures, spin-offs, and recapitalizations, all of which take away the
kinds of financial or organizational changes private equity used
to bring to the table. Union power and membership have dimin-
ished, freeing companies to engage in layoffs and workforce
reductions, which became common in the eighties and nineties,
and remain so. As Steven Kaplan, a close observer of buyouts over
the past thirty years, put it in 1997: "We are all Henry Kravis now."

Another, related explanation for private equity's ability to
create value is that private equity firms add managerial expertise to the companies they buy. Again, there may have been
some truth to this as a general matter in the 1980s, and it may
remain true for mid-cap companies that are moving from the
founding generation to the next, or that are divisions being sold
or spun off by larger companies and are not overseen by managers capable of running an independent company. From the
1990s on, too, smaller private equity funds have specialized by
industry, making it possible they might combine change-agent
willpower with expertise of value to such businesses.

Yet it is far from clear why expertise needs to be linked
to whole-company buyouts. Management consulting firms,
investment banks, human resources departments, and search
firms can and routinely do supply knowledge and talent where
needed. The best-paid private equity professionals receive
among the highest compensation available, but so, too, do managers of public companies, due to the shift to stock and option

86   compensation private equity firms helped stimulate. No evident labor market failure could justify the scale of the modern private equity industry.

For the overall private equity industry, the best current publicly palatable explanation of its success is that private equity's value consists in its financial specialization and economies of scale. The largest private equity firms' creditworthiness and reputation (to creditors), and their "incestuous" network of relationships with other financial institutions, gives them an advantage in financing business. Private equity adds value in the same way J. P. Morgan did a hundred years ago. In other words, private equity firms are, in effect, banks—albeit ones that do not take deposits or directly make loans.

Companies needing debt capital can of course raise it on their own, by going to banks and the capital markets. But for any given company, such capital transactions are typically unusual, happening once every five years or longer. Private equity firms, by contrast, are constantly in the flow of capital markets, both for debt and equity. The largest of them continuously engage in raising new funds, liquidating investments, borrowing to finance new deals, paying down or refinancing debt, and working through bankruptcies caused by the debt they use. Private equity firms are classic repeat players in highly institutionalized financial markets, where seemingly minor informational differences can translate into large cash flow impacts. As one researcher has concluded:

> Simply put, private equity's primary contribution to US firms today appears to be cheap debt financing, rather than governance, strategy, and operations.

What makes this explanation plausible is that after 1990, a
new capital market emerged, critical to private equity in operation: the leveraged loan market. The junk bonds that in the
eighties helped buyouts become viable at large scale suffered
reputational harm from overreach. While high-yield debt—as
junk bonds are called by their friends—returned, it was increasingly displaced by risky loans from banks.

Faced with higher capital requirements coming out of the
bank crisis of the early nineties, banks began to increase their
off-loading of risk through syndications: they would originate
loans but then effectively sell them to others. The buyers
included not only other banks, but insurance companies, hedge
funds, collateralized debt obligation issuers, and other institutions. Private equity firms are embedded in flows of information
and transactions that position them well to shave the interest
rates of the debt they raise. Bonds are governed by the securities
laws and the SEC; leveraged loans are legally exempt from securities laws. This means that loan placements do not trigger disclosure requirements in the securities laws, the leveraged loan
market is not policed by the SEC, and rules against insider
trading do not apply.

Despite data limits, some research bears on whether private
equity adds value. Overall, studies point to three conclusions.
First, buyout returns are cyclical, as are public company returns,
suggesting private equity firms never had an overall ability to
outperform, as the better governance story would suggest.
Second, relatedly, private equity is riskier than appreciated, so
its risk-adjusted returns are only just adequate, or perhaps
worse. Third, even if private equity did outperform public companies in the eighties, they no longer do so, especially net of

88 fees. One study finds private equity performance as reported publicly reflects inflated valuations, that average net-of-fee raw performance was 3 percent below the S&P 500, and when risk-adjusted, underperformance was 6 percent per year, even as private equity firms earned 6 percent per year in fees. A 2016 study, relying on confidential return data from private equity fund investors, concludes:

> Average buyout fund returns ... before 2006 have exceeded ... public markets ... [but] post-2005 ... returns have been roughly equal to those of public markets.

The bottom line for investors is that private equity investments simply break even. If so, their broader effects on society as a whole become all the more important to understand and assess.

The Effects of Private Equity on Society Generally

Here we encounter the same obstacle that confronts testing whether and how private equity funds add value. Opacity blocks reliable and replicable evaluations of private equity's overall social effects. If investors are no better off, and private equity achieves break-even results by generating what economists call negative externalities—that is, harms to third parties—then the private equity legitimacy deficit created by private equity's darkness would rightly grow.

Even if public disclosure itself creates costs, lack of disclosure can hide, and may well induce, social harms. Hidden information impedes existing competition and reduces entry by new competitors. Consumers pay more in dark markets than in an open market, reducing social welfare. Darkness can hide numerous specific harms that journalists and researchers currently have to spend significant effort investigating at private equity–owned companies to uncover, such as: fraud, poor working conditions, wage reductions, customer overcharges, elder abuse, health-and-safety violations, government corruption, toxic emissions, greenhouse gas emissions, and even human rights abuses. Some of these harms may be the product of negligent or inattentive managers. But some may actually reflect transfers of value to private equity firms or their investors. If so, they are not virtues sensible business leaders discuss in public.

If one had to predict private equity's overall social impact, it would also be mixed, and would vary depending on the goods or services a private equity–owned business produces, and how it is governed by law and regulation. Recall that private equity debt, compensation, and governance create sharp incentives to maximize cash flow. Cash can increase from greater revenues or lower costs. Costs are easier to cut than revenues are to increase, and labor costs are easiest to cut. Without legal offsets, it is often cheaper for an employer to fire some workers and rehire others than to retrain existing workers, even if retraining would be better for employees. Private equity is particularly likely to be hazardous to employees in the US, where they have weak legal entitlements (the weakest of all countries assessed by the Organization for Economic Cooperation and Development), including underpriced unemployment insurance, and are no longer meaningfully protected by labor law or unions. Labor and taxpayers, who subsidize some of the costs of job loss, are

90   generally likely to lose from greater private equity dominance of the economy.

What about consumers? Private equity is likely to benefit consumers of search goods—goods or services whose value is apparent before sale—because profits will follow. By contrast, private equity is more likely to harm consumers of credence goods—healthcare, legal services, and higher education, for example—where consumers remain uncertain about quality, and over- and under-diagnosis and treatment are typical. In between, for experience goods, where quality is only known after purchase, outcomes may vary depending on how willing and able consumers are to switch among sellers.

More generally, private equity's temptation to over-cut costs will be mitigated where enforcement of regulation is rapid and effective, but not where it is slow or spotty. Where law creates a well-calibrated system of penalties and enforcement, private equity–owned businesses are likely to invest in effective control systems and to be less likely than other businesses to impose costs on third parties. Where, however, law is either poorly designed or weakly enforced, or where it is incapable of being well calibrated (as with credence good markets), or where it can be gamed, owing to uncertain specification (for example in instance where law tends to rely on standards rather than rules), private equity–owned businesses are more likely to impose costs on third parties.

If this analysis is right, private equity firms would be most threatening to social order in regulated industries, such as public utilities or infrastructure, or where traditional approaches to social protection have—due to the necessity of experience-based judgments by service providers—depended on professional cultures and self-regulation. Again, examples that jump to mind include healthcare and higher education. If one thinks the US legal and enforcement systems work well, then one would expect private equity to improve social outcomes; if one thinks the systems work poorly, or are getting worse over time, one would have the opposite expectation.

In terms of its effects on wealth inequality, private equity is simpler to assess. It is an important way that differential access to investment options concentrates wealth over time. After buyouts, private equity firms reduce employment and create significant levels of job turnover, reduce hourly wages relative to revenues, and destabilize communities that are dependent on durable jobs. They are tax-favored in ways that are hard to defend. Their ownership is also concentrated. Stephen Schwarzman, for example, CEO of Blackstone, which has a market value of $116 billion as of this writing, owns about 20 percent of its equity. Henry Kravis and George Roberts together own 34 percent of the combined equity of KKR, with its market value of $49 billion. The three leaders of Carlyle, valued as of this writing at $12 billion, own either 30 percent, 35 percent, or 43 percent of its stock, depending on how shares are counted. The gap between what private equity owners get and what their companies pay employees is likely enormous, but not publicly reported.

For perspective, public companies have moved in the same direction as private equity firms since the 1980s, due to market pressures and legal changes. Similarly, top earnings in the US in law, sports, and investment banking have increased dramatically in the last twenty years. At the same time, overall wage growth has barely kept pace, and the US has experienced

92   massive increases in wealth disparities, extensively documented by Thomas Piketty. Researchers have found that private equity buyouts contribute to job polarization—that is, growth of employment in high-skill jobs (such as management and technical positions) and low-skill jobs (such as food-service and janitorial work) along with a decline in middle-skill jobs (such as clerical, construction, manufacturing, and retail occupations).

Piketty attributes the explosion at the top of the US and UK income distribution to evolution in social norms in corporate governance, which had held executive compensation in check. Buyouts and private equity firms (and their academic cheerleaders) were among the forces that set the stage for that norm shift, along with globalization and hostile takeovers.

Private equity also directly contributes to those disparities as part of the system of US corporate governance. Political activity by public companies and private equity firms has changed tax law, antitrust law, labor law, and regulation overall in ways that have enhanced disparities. No one can fairly dispute that private equity activities are a powerful force contributing not only to overall economic growth (as their defenders stress) but also to the income and wealth gaps that have accompanied economic growth over the past fifty years.

In sum, private equity seems now to derive its profits primarily from its central role in capital markets. As with financial institutions in the past, private equity's role reflects economies of scale. The larger private equity complexes become, the more central they are to flows of capital. Through club deals, secondary buyouts, and lobbying through trade groups, they function less like rivals than allies. The more they are in the flow, the more they know about capital and product markets, the more readily they can put informational and relational advantages to work. Meanwhile, the businesses they control remain private—shielded from scrutiny by financial rivals, product competitors, regulators, and the public.

While private equity funds do not have the same economies of scale as index funds, massive funds of $5 billion or more now make up more than half of private equity fundraising. The largest complexes are growing larger, globally, faster than public companies or the economy overall. They and their political allies wield significant political influence. The drama that sometimes accompanies buyouts, coupled with lack of transparency, make them even more threatening to the American public than index funds. No less than index funds, private equity funds create—and face—a problem of twelve.

The Politics and Political Risks of the Problem of Twelve (So Far)

Public companies were a core part of the economy and government in the middle part of the twentieth century. They were legitimated by war, securities law, progressive taxation, labor unions, and regulation. But from 1970 on, they changed and were changed by politics and economics.

Corporate leaders invested in their own political capital, and applied the resulting power to reduce the constraints of antitrust law, taxation, and regulation, and, most importantly, to lay low what had been one of their most powerful political rivals—private sector labor unions. In the same period, however, public companies' economic freedom dramatically shrank. Indeed, they faced an existential crisis—in the form of globalization, inflation, automation, hostile takeovers, and buyouts. Since 1990, they have also faced an ongoing challenge in the form of a shareholder rights movement, in which institutional investors—first public pension funds and hedge funds, and lately index funds—organized politically to reduce their autonomy. Meanwhile, the private equity industry, which seemed to diminish in the recession of 1989–91, has more than recovered and has been growing much faster than the public equity markets, displacing public companies in both the economy and the political system.

Today, index funds and private equity funds are themselves politically active and influential, and other political actors—civil society organizations, social activists, and political parties and politicians themselves—have responded to these funds' growing economic clout and political power. Index funds have become increasingly politically influential on issues such as diversity, treatment of workers, and climate change, drawing charges of socialism from the right, and of antitrust harm and of dragging their feet on other issues, such as corporate political disclosure, from the left. Private equity funds, by contrast, are drawing a veil over more sectors of the economy, partly by leveraging politically controversial tax breaks, partly by continuing the suppression of labor and increasing wealth disparities, and partly by simply doing an excellent job at whatever private for-profit business can do—whether it's satisfying or defrauding consumers, increasing productivity and innovation, or imposing negative consequences on unwitting third parties.

The Contemporary Setting for Index Funds and Private Equity Funds in the Political Arena

Berle-and-Means public companies remain politically organized and active. They are no longer threatened by socialism internationally or labor domestically, nor are they strongly constrained by antitrust law. They have, compared to the mid-twentieth century, reduced taxes (even lower after further cuts under Donald Trump) and regulation, particularly economic

96   regulation. Free market ideas are far more prevalent in policy debates than they were in 1965. Nixonian wage-and-price controls are not even being considered in the post-COVID inflationary spike. The primary constraints on business are no longer government or labor, but market-aligned shareholder governance.

Much of government regulation remains in force, if weakened. Workers' compensation, minimum wage laws, and unemployment insurance remain, if effectively reduced by inflation. Workplace and safety rules persist, if erratically enforced. Environmental regulations continue, if only weakly updated to reflect climate change. Corporations do pay taxes, and plan around tax law. Federal securities laws—and the transparency, legitimacy, and accountability they create for big business—remain largely intact as applied to public companies.

Some sixties-era organized political adversaries—consumer groups, human rights organizations, and left-leaning think tanks—continue to press for laws contrary to business interests. The same is true at times of both political parties: Democrats more so, but Republicans, too, on issues such as diversity and immigration (where large companies are generally more open to cosmopolitanism and free movement of labor than the Republican Party). But Democrats since Clinton have been far more openly and consistently pro-business than they were in the middle of the twentieth century, and Republicans continue to be strongly anti-tax and, on most business issues, anti-regulation.

In sum, the policy state for large companies has markedly improved since 1970. Companies are used to winning in the domestic political sphere.

At the same time, they lack public trust and legitimacy, and this forces them to find allies or work through channels such as litigation, highly technical laws, and regulatory appointments that much of the voting public does not track. Public companies have been increasingly regulated by a new organized opposition group: shareholders generally, institutional shareholders in particular, and increasingly index funds above all others. No longer can the presumptive passivity of dispersed shareholders of Berle-and-Means companies be taken for granted. Institutional shareholders are a new political force, acting both in struggles for control over individual companies, but also more generally. The number of anti-management shareholder resolutions increased from fewer than 40 in 1987 to 153 in 1991, or about one proposal at every forty-two US public companies. In 2022, there were 797 such proposals, or roughly one proposal for every eight companies, and among the S&P 500 (the largest public companies), each year each company receives at least one proposal, on average.

In 1990 alone, "more shareholder proposals passed . . . than in the entire history of shareholder proposals prior to 1990." Most recently, the number of approved proposals has jumped markedly, from 1 percent over the period from 2010 to 2019 to 12.4 percent in 2020 and 19.2 percent in 2021. Since most companies who anticipate losing give in and settle, the impact of these resolutions has been ever larger than these numbers suggest. Gerald Davis and Tracy Thompson have argued that the shareholder rights movement's rapid success—from its creation in 1985 to significant political influence by 1990—suggests how important growth in institutional ownership was from 1960 to 1990.

98   The consequence of corporate political success in the 1970s, and the emergence of shareholders as a political force in the 1980s, is that index funds and private equity funds have emerged as political organizations in a political landscape significantly altered from what it was in the mid-twentieth century. Without labor as a force, with business lacking public trust, and with government itself weak, the potential power of index funds and private equity funds is significant. More than any other types of organizations, they have power to rival that of big business generally, in a moment that is starkly different, if no less dangerous for democracy and capitalism, than the 1920s and 1930s.

      The comfortable corporate alliances with labor of the mid-twentieth century are gone. Many features of the New Deal that helped legitimate capitalism and business generally have been eliminated or reduced. The transparency imposed on public companies by securities laws remains largely intact, but only for companies not owned by private equity firms. US businesses as a whole survived globalization and automation, but only by becoming global, coming to rely on contractors who lack job security and employer-based benefits, and offshoring increasing amounts of work to geographically remote polities. In so doing, they have lost much of their legitimacy in the eyes of the American public, even as they remain vulnerable to hostile takeovers and shareholder activism.

      As a result, the perception is that corporate leaders are increasingly detached from ground-level US politics. Public opinion of large companies is at an all-time low. Populism is not confined to the left—it helped elect Donald Trump. In this moment, public companies are under threat from index funds and private equity funds, in different ways. Index funds threaten directly to build their influence over public companies, in part because broader segments of the public are channeling their money and efforts into governance via such funds. Meanwhile, private equity funds threaten to supplant public companies altogether, taking them private and outside of both index fund ownership and SEC disclosure rules. In turn, both types of funds are under political pressure themselves. Index funds are being attacked by Republicans as socialist tools; private equity funds are being attacked by Democrats as tools of plutocracy.

The Political Influence of Index Funds and Private Equity Funds

As index funds and private equity funds have grown, they have become increasingly politically active and influential. Some of their influence activities are defensive—they are under increasing threat from political entrepreneurs and public skepticism, thanks to the power they are amassing, or are perceived already to have. In this way, their political influence and their political vulnerability are related—both come from their sheer scale, which gives them financial influence and resources that can overmatch most other organizations in their capacity for action and power.

How do index funds exercise political influence? They mostly do so indirectly, as owners of large blocks of corporate shares. Because they own an increasing share of all large public companies, they influence much of the economy. They can use their votes as shareholders to affect mergers, board elections, and the outcome of shareholder resolutions. They can use their power to ensure that corporations' top executives will answer

100   their calls, take meetings with them, and engage with them on a range of issues. They work to put policy issues on the public agenda, to influence how regulations are shaped, and to respond to company-specific choices and crises. By influencing companies, they influence the economy, and the way that elected officials govern. Even if Congress or the SEC or some other agency does not mandate that companies behave in a certain way, index funds can pressure companies to act that way. Corporate governance can be—and increasingly has become—a substitute for ordinary political governance.

Contrary to the popular impression that only eccentric gadflies attack companies at shareholder meetings, 80 percent of shareholder proposals on social topics (that is, proposals not focused specifically on how companies are governed) are initiated by organizations, not individuals. The organizations do not typically include index funds. Instead, they include public pension funds, religious organizations (nuns are quite active), charities, social impact funds (mutual funds set up to have a political impact), and a range of civil society organizations that have partly substituted for labor unions in the course of their long decline in American politics. Labor organizations also propose issues for shareholder votes, but they bring fewer than 10 percent of all proposals. Most proposals come from the left, but conservative organizations have also brought hundreds of proposals. Index funds increasingly determine the outcomes of votes on these proposals.

Many of these proposals have clear and broad political resonance. The top issues, making up over half of shareholder resolutions, are diversity, climate change, and corporate political activity. Each generates huge grassroots energy outside the corporate sphere, in ordinary politics. Other votes concern a litany of modern political issues: the Israeli-Palestinian conflict, animal abuse, plastic bottle use, income inequality, facial recognition technology: the list goes on. On all of these topics, popular energy has been channeled into corporate governance. Index funds have chosen or been forced to take political stands.

An example is State Street's promotion of gender and other forms of diversity. Racial and gender equality have been flashpoints in politics throughout American history, and they remain at the core of the culture wars that divide the US political parties. Increasingly, global US public companies have had diversity forced upon them through the inevitably racially and ethnically diverse employment that offshoring implies, and through the capitalist need to cater to markets beyond white American middle-class men.

But index funds have been pushing companies toward genuine diversity, at the highest levels, even more emphatically than globalization demands. State Street—principally a custody bank, handling back office functions for a variety of Wall Street firms—is perhaps the leading example. It has for many years publicly pursued diversity as one of its own corporate goals.

With great ceremony, for example, it commissioned *Fearless Girl* in 2017—a statue of a girl standing with her hands on her hips—adorned with a plaque reading "Know the power of women in leadership. SHE makes a difference." *Fearless Girl* was initially sited on Bowling Green near Wall Street, opposite the *Charging Bull* statue, a symbol of the wealth-generating capacity of financial markets. *Fearless Girl* now sits directly opposite the New York Stock Exchange.

102   State Street's diversity messaging can also be found on its public-facing website:

"With employees around the world, we know that our differences are what make us a stronger company. We are committed to developing an environment that offers equal opportunities to individuals with distinctive backgrounds and unique perspectives. There is belongingness in inclusion, growth in diversity, and fairness in equity." As a privately owned public company, State Street is entitled to pursue diversity in recruitment and staffing decisions. But because it also owns major blocks of stock in most other public companies, its own corporate values have implications for the broader corporate universe.

State Street's 2021 Stewardship Report notes that "Alongside our call on gender diversity, this year we increasingly focused on addressing systemic racial inequality." It reports 220 corporate "engagements" on the topic. SHE is the ticker symbol for an index fund State Street created to invest in companies that "demonstrate greater gender diversity within senior leadership than other firms in their sector." State Street has published diversity guidelines expecting "all companies in our portfolio to offer public disclosures" on diversity, including "board oversight," "strategy," "goals," "metrics," and "board diversity."

State Street's efforts go beyond jawboning. As its guidance document plainly states, it will use its voting power to back up its words: "If a company . . . does not disclose the racial and ethnic composition of its board, we will vote against the Chair of the Nominating Committee." More specifically, State Street notes, "If a company . . . does not have at least one director from an underrepresented racial or ethnic community, we will vote against the Chair of the Nominating Committee." On gender, "Beginning in the 2023 proxy season, we will expect companies . . . to have boards comprised of at least 30 percent women directors."

State Street, in other words, is pushing companies to go beyond the requirements of the most aggressive US law yet adopted on board gender diversity—California's 2018 requirement that by 2022 stock exchange–listed corporations headquartered in the state have at least two or three female directors. State Street's efforts, moreover, are ongoing, while California's law was struck down as violating the state's equal protection clause in 2022.

With pressure of this kind from an array of institutional investors beyond index funds, public company board diversity practices have significantly increased in recent years. As the Conference Board recently reported, "24 percent of the S&P 500 disclosed the racial composition of their boards in 2020," and more than twice as many (59 percent) "did so in 2021." Women's share of seats on boards of the large companies in the S&P 500 has increased significantly, from 20 percent in 2016, to 29 percent in 2021; among companies in the broader Russell 3000 index, it rose to 24 percent in 2021. Racial diversity lags gender diversity, but it, too, is increasing.

Diversity efforts remain politically divisive, and beliefs among investors, academic researchers, and ideological activists divide sharply over the topic. Many believe diversity is aligned with the profit motive, and that there is a compelling business case for increased diversity on corporate boards and

104   senior leadership teams. For example, private equity firm Carlyle—not known in the same way as State Street for publicly supporting diversity—reports:

> The average earnings growth of Carlyle portfolio companies with two or more diverse board members has been nearly 12% per year greater than the average of companies that lack diversity. . . . After controlling for industry, fund, and vintage year, companies with diverse boards generate earnings growth that's five times faster, on average, with each diverse board member associated with a 5% increase in annualized earnings growth.

In 2020 the Nasdaq exchange adopted a comply or explain standard (which the SEC approved the next year), requiring companies listed on that exchange to disclose whether they have a diverse board, or explain why not. Right-leaning think-tank activists and academics called the proposal "immoral" and "progressive social engineering." The legality of the listing standard is the subject of a pending federal court challenge brought by two conservative impact litigation groups and nearly twenty red-state attorneys general. They argue that the Nasdaq's standard imposes a quota system, despite its requiring companies to do nothing other than disclose their reasons for having a non-diverse board.

Supporting the Nasdaq standard is not only Nasdaq itself, a for-profit business not generally organized to pursue political goals, but also a coalition of Nasdaq-listed companies. An amicus brief filed by the corporate law firm Wachtell, Lipton, Rosen & Katz on behalf of nearly 120 retired judges, SEC officials, business lawyers, and legal academics argued that the "freedom for private actors like the stock exchanges to innovate in corporate governance and disclosure is an intended feature of [the US] system of corporate and securities laws, and an important reason for the success of [US] capital markets." Also supporting the goals of the Nasdaq standard are the Big Three index fund sponsors, Vanguard, BlackRock, and State Street.

Opponents of the rule argue:

> Return-seeking investors have different interests around these proposed rules than asset managers, particularly index fund operators. Index fund managers are likely to benefit financially from Nasdaq's diversity rules, even if they have no effect on stock prices . . . [because t]hey facilitate governance activism . . . to attract assets from . . . socially minded millennials and pension fund stewards. This in turn increases managers' fees.

In other words, argue such critics, support of diversity by index funds is a conflict of interest, in which fund sponsors subordinate corporate and overall investor interests to favor a subset of investors who are sensitive to the politics of diversity. Unexplained by these critics is why, if diversity were bad for investors, or just bad, index fund support for diversity would not drive away investors who do not support diversity, or only want to maximize profits. Whatever one's overall opinion about this conflict, it is undeniable that it illustrates how index funds both exert influence in, and are entangled by, complex and inescapably political debates.

In 2010, the Supreme Court in *Citizens United v. Federal Election Commission* reversed multiple precedents and permitted corporate managers to start spending corporate funds freely in federal election campaigns. In doing so, the court followed Lewis Powell's infamous playbook, written in 1971 for the Chamber of Commerce. It departed from normal procedure, invented a fictional history for how corporations functioned in the newly independent United States of America, and flouted its own interpretive norms to use the First Amendment to strike down campaign finance laws not simply as applied to the expressive nonprofit that sued, but for all companies. Its premises—that public companies somehow speak on behalf of thousands of dispersed shareholders—were obscure at best, but its political implications were clear. Justice Anthony Kennedy, in writing for the majority, presumed that corporate political expenditures would be disclosed. Justice Kennedy was apparently unaware that no political spending disclosure requirement existed in corporate or securities law.

The shock of the decision—viewed unfavorably by 80 percent of Americans, including a majority of Republican voters—led to attempts to require public companies to disclose their political spending. Such disclosure had previously been less important, since spending had only been permitted in state and local elections and in referendum campaigns. Disclosure was also a part of the Republican Party program, the basis for advocating for the weakening of campaign finance laws. For decades, conservatives who opposed most forms of campaign-finance regulation argued for a system of unlimited spending with full disclosure. For example, during a controversy over the national political parties' use of unregulated soft money during the 1990s, conservative columnist George Will proposed boiling down campaign finance regulation to just "seven words: no cash, full disclosure, no foreign money." Similarly, the *Wall Street* *Journal* editorial board wrote in 2000: "Our view is that the Constitution allows consenting adults to give as much as they want to whomever they want, subject to disclosure on the Internet."

After *Citizens United* freed companies to spend in elections, debates over corporate political disclosure became newly political, and partisan. Public Citizen, a consumer advocacy group founded in 1971 by Ralph Nader to lobby for campaign finance regulations, began to push for a legislative or regulatory response. Meanwhile, George Will, and other Republicans, unashamedly reversed their commitment to disclosure. Democrat-backed bills were blocked by Republican filibusters in the Senate. Ultimately, Congress failed to act. Academics petitioned the SEC to require political disclosure, but before the SEC could bring itself to do so, Republicans in Congress began inserting budget riders to block such action by the SEC, and placed sufficient priority on that interest that the Democratic leadership was and has remained unwilling to negotiate for the riders' removal. As a result, public companies can freely spend their shareholders' money in federal elections without being required to disclose how much or how they are doing so.

These developments alarmed investors who were already focused on how politics could be crucial to corporate strategy, making corporate political activity an important risk factor in valuing corporations and monitoring corporate managers. Researchers also noted that managers could use corporate funds to pursue their personal interests by contributing to political campaigns with an eye toward taking political office in the future—and, indeed, 11 percent of the CEOs in 2000 who had retired by 2011 served in political positions after retiring. More generally, in most industries, observable political activity—PAC donations and reported lobbying—correlates negatively with measures of shareholder power and value, demonstrating the risk that corporate political expenditures could simply be a waste of resources and, worse, a distraction for senior managers from ordinary business.

Frustrated in Washington, shareholders increased a pre-existing campaign to pressure companies individually to disclose their political activities. The Center for Political Accountability, founded in 2003, had been tracking and reporting on such disclosures, and had developed model shareholder resolutions that began to be presented for votes at annual meetings. By the time of *Citizens United*, eighty-five companies had adopted some variation of a policy provided by the Center in which they pledged to disclose their electioneering activities. By 2020, the number had risen to 240.

Between 2010 and 2020, shareholders of large US public companies were repeatedly asked to support resolutions asking companies to disclose their political activity. Overall, shareholder support rose steadily during that period, with resolutions also achieving majority support at an increasing rate over time. In 2021, forty-two such proposals went to a vote, ten were passed with majority votes, and the average support level was 41 percent—all-time highs.

How have institutional shareholders generally, and index funds in particular, voted in response to such proposals? In contrast to their stances on diversity and climate, index funds have been laggards on political spending disclosure. As late as 2019, only one of the four largest index fund sponsors, State Street, had supported a standard disclosure resolution. This contrasts with support from other institutions, such as those following guidelines that call for companies to disclose annually the amounts and the recipients of all political and charitable contributions, as well as any expenditures earmarked for such activities provided through a third party.

The reluctance of the other index fund sponsors may finally be giving way—but not at the same rate. In 2021, BlackRock and Vanguard backed the Center for Political Accountability's model disclosure proposal for the first time, with BlackRock doing so at half of the twelve companies where the issue was up for a vote, and Vanguard in three. State Street increased its support level from 46 percent in 2020 to 75 percent in 2021. Fidelity remained at the bottom of major index fund sponsors, but did vote in favor of one resolution.

By voting for some but not all political spending disclosure proposals, index fund sponsors are taking an approach they have taken on other political issues: linking their votes to specific facts, not a general stance. For example, 38 percent of shareholders, but not Vanguard, voted in favor in 2021 of a political spending proposal at Flowers Foods, a nationwide US bakery company selling Wonder Bread, Nature's Own, and Dave's Killer Bread. As justification, Vanguard said, politics is less important in baking than to other industries. (Flowers has sponsored a PAC for over twenty-five years and mentions regulation more than fifty times in its most recent annual report, in which it also acknowledges its dependency on energy supplies, which it notes are subject to political risk, along with labor and supply chains, also subject to acknowledged political risks. The company has 1,000 unionized employees, out of 9,000.)

110   Then, in 2022, Vanguard changed its vote to yes. Vanguard noted that after the 2021 vote, it encouraged Flowers to disclose more so that shareholders could assess its board's oversight of political risk, but Flowers changed nothing about its political disclosures. In the lead-up to the 2021 meeting, Flowers provided no information to Vanguard on the topic, though it agreed to include politics in an upcoming assessment that all public companies have to perform as part of their annual compliance with SEC reporting rules. Perhaps most importantly, Vanguard noted that Flowers managers "acknowledged that [corporate political activity] is an important part of their strategy," contradicting the prior rationale for its decision to vote no on the disclosure resolution.

Index funds also exert direct political influence. Each major index fund complex now has a substantial public and government relations staff. They write long comment letters on proposed regulations, attend conferences dedicated to issues they care about, and directly lobby elected officials and their staffs. Their support for an idea for a new regulation, or a listing standard being considered by the stock exchanges, can significantly increase the odds of the idea's adoption. Their opposition makes a proposal harder for officials to push through.

All three of the biggest index fund complexes are part of the Investment Company Institute, a trade group that participates in Washington, DC, debates and occasionally files court cases on behalf of its members' interests. The institute has an annual budget of $65 million and a staff of 180. In 2021, it published thirty-five reports, more than three hundred statistical releases, and a continuous blog. The institute sponsors a PAC, which in the 2022 election cycle gave more than \$1 million. It has consistently given \$4 to \$6 million per year over the last twenty-five years in disclosed lobbying funds, to often fifty or more lobbyists.

Index funds represent only a small number of the thousands of funds represented by the institute, which is not always able or willing to advance policies for the benefit of index funds. Nonetheless, since the institute charges dues based on assets under management, index funds have the same large and increasing potential influence on the Investment Company Institute as they do on public companies. At a minimum, they are likely to be able to block the institute from taking positions that are adverse to their interests. The ICI has at times presented information to the world that minimizes the scale and potential influence of index fund complexes.

Beyond the Investment Company Institute, each of the index fund complexes conducts its own lobbying and public relations activity. Each of BlackRock, State Street, Vanguard, and Fidelity has spent \$1 to \$5 million a year on lobbyists for more than a decade, totaling more disclosed lobbying expenditures and more lobbyists than the institute. Lobbying disclosures are coarse and unrevealing, but it should not be surprising that the index fund lobbyists have included regulation of asset management among the issues on which they focus.

Consistent with their somewhat different corporate cultures, the large index fund complexes have participated differently in politics. Vanguard, lacking public shareholders, has tended to be less public and visible in its efforts, although it does routinely engage with congressional staff about pending bills.

112   Fidelity, owned by a single family, has also been circumspect. State Street, a public company but one with most of its revenues derived from services not directly related to index fund sponsorship, has tended to focus on other political issues.

That has left BlackRock, out of the Big Four, as the most prominent political actor. It has not shied from the task. When antitrust and finance scholarship began to appear in the late 2010s suggesting that ownership by index funds and other large institutional owners could lead to antitrust harms by their portfolio companies, BlackRock's representatives were loud critics of the scholarship. BlackRock attended conferences, published white papers, and hired lobbyists to meet with politicians to influence how the scholarship was being received.

Index funds must attend to the social goals of many investors, in order to attract them to invest. ESG-style investing—investing based on environmental, social, and governance goals—is increasingly done through ESG-based indexes, and ESG-based funds are the fastest growing segment of retail asset management. The term ESG was first popularized in the early 2000s following the publication of a UN report called "Who Cares Wins," collectively produced by a group of multinational financial institutions. Since then, the acronym has become an umbrella term for messaging by the public, investors, or corporate managers toward what used to be called corporate responsibility. That term dates to the 1950s, or socially responsible investing, which can be traced at least to the South Africa divestment movement of the 1980s. It had even earlier antecedents, but became more widespread in the 1990s.

Since the UN report, ESG has become an increasingly important way for companies and investors to orient their

actual behavior. "The one-year growth rate of ESG fund launches
[in 2021] in the United States is more than twice that of funds
without, 80 percent versus 34 percent," one report noted. Index
funds respond to demand for socially responsible investing in
part by pursuing political goals.

ESG investing's growth has clear implications for index
funds. Not only have they increasingly introduced ESG-based
indexes, but the values being pursued by ESG funds have
become important influences on how standard index funds and
their sponsors use their potential political influence. The biggest issue that involves long-term thinking, of course, is climate change, where index funds and their leaders have been
particularly influential and controversial, not only in company-
level governance, of the kind discussed earlier, but in speaking
publicly about climate policy itself.

When Larry Fink—CEO of the largest index fund complex,
BlackRock—speaks on public policy issues, everyone listens.
His annual letters are designed to, and do, generate immediate
media coverage, and his views are analyzed carefully by the
investment community and those working for public company
boards. Politicians and policymakers are affected. Politicians
cannot afford to ignore important ideological shifts that are
driving capital market activity.

At a high level, Fink has endorsed the big idea that
"Capitalism has the power to shape society and act as a powerful catalyst for change." "To prosper over time," Fink argues,
"every company must not only deliver financial performance,
but also show how it makes a positive contribution to society."
More directly: "climate risk is investment risk." In the two years
since Fink made that statement, we have seen "a tectonic shift

114   of capital" with "sustainable investments . . . now reach[ing] $4 trillion," as he notes in his 2022 letter to CEOs. Only a small part of that shift is attributable to Fink's public statements. But the shift is so large—indeed so much larger than the climate subsidies in the Inflation Reduction Act of 2022—that BlackRock's influence is still significant, driving capital allocation to green businesses, and along with it, politics and policy.

The shift in capital partly stimulated by BlackRock helped build a foundation for the SEC's pending rule proposal on climate-related disclosure by public companies. BlackRock filed a twenty-two-page comment letter generally supporting the SEC's proposed rule. BlackRock reiterated its support for "mandatory climate-related disclosures," and reaffirmed BlackRock's belief in "the relevance of climate risk to investors' decision-making processes." It also supported quantitative disclosures aligned with the Greenhouse Gas Protocol. While BlackRock offered some criticisms of the ways it thought the proposal went too far, overall its support lends credibility to Fink's public messaging about BlackRock's seeing climate risk as investment risk, and adds to momentum to the SEC proposal. BlackRock's endorsements reflect another channel for political influence by index fund sponsors—networking and partnerships with civil society organizations active in the policy space.

Through its comment letter, BlackRock lent its weight to this corporate governance and public policy cause. In doing so, it was taking positions contrary to those of some public companies and prominent business trade groups. The comment letter filed by the US Chamber of Commerce, for example, says that the rule is "vast and unprecedented in [its] scope, complexity, rigidity and

prescriptive particularity, and exceed[s] the bounds of the SEC's
lawful authority." Oil company Continental Resources argued the
proposal goes beyond the SEC's constitutional authority and that
existing disclosure requirements were sufficient.

Many other public companies, even from the oil and gas
sector, support the SEC proposal. Occidental Petroleum's
comment letter states, "We support the Commission's objective to improve the consistency, comparability and reliability
of climate-related disclosures and provide investors with
decision-useful information regarding climate change metrics."
It may be precisely when policy and politics divide business
groups and shareholder groups that the political influence of
the index funds is at its greatest.

BlackRock is aware of and manages the political risks it
runs while engaging on climate change. Its CEO, Larry Fink, is
reported to have directly told the governance teams working at
his firm to "do a better job explaining their votes to company
executives . . . particularly around climate-related proposals,"
out of a "concern . . . [over] public perception . . . that BlackRock
had gone too far in pushing an environmental agenda." In 2022,
as Republicans' use of ESG as a talking point in their fundraising
and speechifying was on the rise, BlackRock's support for
climate-related shareholder proposals fell.

BlackRock attributed the drop to the specifics of the proposals, which it said involved more micromanagement than in
past years. In hitting back at its Republican critics, whom
BlackRock accuses of "inaccurate statements about BlackRock's
motive for participating in various ESG-related initiatives,"
BlackRock simultaneously emphasized that it continued to

own hundreds of billions of dollars of oil and gas company investments, while also believing that climate change is a real threat—and a real financial opportunity.

As with diversity and corporate political activity, there are differences among index fund sponsors on climate. Vanguard's comment letter on the SEC climate disclosure proposal was a notch less supportive than BlackRock's. It implies that the rule as proposed should not be approved. It also signals the SEC should trust companies to judge themselves on the importance of climate, an approach that invites underreporting. Vanguard's letter is just far enough above the line of support to not generate significant climate-activist backlash, while also providing political cover with Republicans and the Chamber of Commerce.

Whether the governor of Texas approves of it or not, and even if Vanguard or other slow-moving institutional owners do not directly insist, most public companies are already making climate-related disclosures. Indeed, by some estimates, 60 percent of the Fortune 500 have made climate commitments, and a sharply rising number have gone as far as making "net zero" commitments. Such companies will continue do to so, because their institutional investors as a whole—accustomed after thirty years of organized exercises of shareholder power—are demanding that information.

Private Equity's Political Influence and Effects

For much of its existence, private equity has not been observably political, in keeping with its overall strategy of remaining private, with as little publicity and transparency into its operations as possible. An exception is that in the 1970s and 1980s, when private equity firms were known as buyout firms, and continuing into the 1990s, they helped lobby (through the National Venture Capital Association) for securities deregulation to make it easier for them to raise capital while remaining private.

Under securities law, none of the companies owned by private equity funds have to report to shareholders, as do public companies. This makes it harder for journalists to identify potential sources of political engagement by those companies or their managers. Many people who have derived their wealth from careers in private equity are rich enough to influence politics without creating observable tracks in the public record. As a result, it is likely that observable political activity understates the industry's actual influence over the political system.

Nonetheless, starting during the financial crisis, private equity firms and their owners began to openly lobby and participate in election campaigns. Since shortly after forming its first formal trade group in the mid-2000s, the industry's lobbying expenditures jumped from relatively low levels to a peak in 2007, as the financial crisis unfolded, as shown in Figure 4.1, which is based on data from Open Secrets. Total lobbying expenditures are now comparable to those of the largest index funds, roughly equivalent to those of hedge funds, and about a fourth that of the US Chamber of Commerce. The industry also donates a large amount of money directly or through conduits to candidates and PACs controlled by parties or candidates.

The crisis led to a major financial reform—the Dodd-Frank Act. Any reform of that magnitude becomes what people in Washington call "a Christmas tree bill," because it is so large that numerous elements can get added to it, like ornaments. Dodd-Frank was likely to have major implications for private

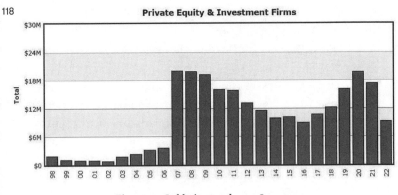

Figure 4.1: Lobbying totals, 1998–2022

equity. Private equity was not significantly responsible for the crisis, but many private equity–funded buyouts failed and many previously acquired companies went bankrupt in its aftermath. Its basic debt-heavy business model and its tight relationships with participants in the leveraged loan market gave it ample reason to engage powerfully in politics during the debates over how government should respond to the crisis. The industry has reason to pay close attention to regulation and law governing finance generally, because the formal legal organization of their funds and advisory firms can be affected by open-ended legal definitions aimed at other financial subsectors, such as hedge funds, investment advisors generally, or investment companies.

Private equity's heavy political engagement continues through today. Open Secrets recently reported that, as early as August 2022, "private equity and hedge fund industries [have] pour[ed] nearly $347.7 million into 2022 midterms." This includes contributions by private equity–sponsored PACs and individual contributions by private equity professionals. The largest recipient—of more than $1 million—was Chuck Schumer. Blackstone alone has contributed $21 million altogether in the current cycle. All four of the other top five private equity firm complexes have been active: KKR, Apollo, and Carlyle, as well as Brookfield, which focuses on real estate.

The effects of private equity contributions and lobbying can be seen in specific policy battles. Private equity—along with its venture capital and hedge fund allies—was able to block yet another attempt, in the Inflation Reduction Act of 2022, to close the carried interest loophole, almost derailing the bill in the process. Kyrsten Sinema was widely reported as the one member of Congress who was only willing to vote for the law if the carried interest reform was deleted. She is among the top recipients of private equity contributions in 2022, and over the last ten years, according to Open Secrets, "Blackstone Group has given the most money to Sinema's political operation."

Private equity has also become politically active in the industry-based regulation of portfolio companies—particularly in professionalized sectors such as healthcare. In 2020, private equity–funded ads almost derailed the No Surprises Act, a rare piece of legislation with widespread bipartisan popular support, which bans the kinds of shockingly high out-of-network medical bills that private equity–owned healthcare providers had exploited in prior years.

This was after having successfully blocked the bill in 2019. In that year, private equity spared no expense in making sure the legislation did not pass. A mysterious group called Doctor Patient Unity launched a campaign in July of 2019 that ultimately spent nearly $54 million. It was later revealed that

Envision, owned by KKR, and TeamHealth, owned by Blackstone, were behind this dark-money campaign. As this episode showed, private equity has become just as adept as businesses generally at using the dark money channels that business lobbies opened up using strategies outlined long ago in the Powell memo.

Private equity firms have their own trade group. Founded in 2006, the Private Equity Council was formed by eleven top private equity firms, later rebranded as the Private Equity Growth Capital Council. The name change highlighted the development that a minority but ever bigger portion of private equity is devoted to investments in growth firms, rather than the mature companies typically targeted in leveraged buyouts. The addition of growth equity investments is a form of financial diversification, but it also helps with public messaging—it makes it possible for the industry to claim that it funds not merely debt-financed, layoff-based buyouts, but also new businesses that create jobs. As the trade group's president said at the time, "Our new name better conveys what private equity is all about: growing companies."

The private equity trade group has recently been rebranded again, as the American Investment Council, fully dispensing with the private equity label. This may reflect sentiment among some private equity managers that the "private" in private equity has unhelpful implications. Jonathan Nelson, head of Providence Equity Partners, said in a television interview: "I think we get off on the wrong track by the name 'private equity.' Honestly, it sounds terrible. In an age of transparency, anything that's private just doesn't sound very good." From 2007 through 2011, the trade group spent an average of $2.8 million per year on lobbying; in 2022, it spent more than $2.9 million on lobbying. Issues it targeted were private equity taxation, partnership audits, the tax deductibility of interest, and symbolic bills attesting that "private equity plays an important role in growing and strengthening ... businesses ... in every State and congressional district."

Representatives of the private equity trade group testify on Capitol Hill. In 2007, one testified at a hearing on "Private Equity's Effects on Workers and Firms," in which he made the case for private equity's contribution to job growth. Although he had to acknowledge that "data on private equity investment's impact on employment in the US is anecdotal," he said that was "a void the [trade group] hopes to fill in time." Another representative testified in another hearing, in 2019, titled "America for Sale? An Examination of the Practices of Private Funds." In his testimony, Drew Maloney emphasized first the role of venture capital and growth equity before turning finally to the buyout portion of the group's membership—but most of the assets under management among the group's members sit in buyout funds.

As with index funds, private equity funds also actively manage their public reputations by investing in favorable research on their industry. As early as the 1980s, KKR was caught misrepresenting the effects of its buyouts on labor in research it funded. The industry trade group pays for research reports touting the industry's contribution to employment. The US Chamber of Commerce, an ally, has opposed draft legislation aimed at regulating private equity, sponsoring reports critical of the bills. The Institute for Private Capital, funded in part by private equity general partners, also sponsors research and roundtables on the industry.

The industry hits back at research conclusions that are not to its liking. In 2018, a research team published a paper showing that private equity–owned dermatology practices perform an unusually high number of well-reimbursed procedures and bill high amounts to Medicare. Within weeks, private equity pressure had led the *Journal of the American Academy of Dermatology* to retract the article—for no given reason, and without any evidence of mistakes.

In contrast to index funds, private equity funds are not participants in the shareholder resolution process. In securities law, widely available participatory governance rights do not exist for companies with a small number of formal legal owners (like a fund), even if the ultimate economic owners of the fund are numerous and dispersed. The politics of going private entail ending dialogue by public investors after a buyout. For a private equity portfolio company, its owners' observable political stance is silence.

But private equity sponsors—the leading private equity companies, as opposed to the companies their funds own— have had no choice but to speak on political topics, including the same kinds of issues on which index funds have been active. Private equity funds have been public proponents of diversity, for example. Is this "virtue signaling"? Unlike index funds, private equity funds do not raise money directly from the general public—their investors are institutions. Some, like public pension funds, care about commitments to diversity. As one law firm that works for private equity has noted, such investors "are placing greater emphasis on diversity . . . and are asking for more information on diversity, equity, and inclusion (DEI) metrics."

Private equity's increasingly global scope also means that the US regulatory framework—which leaves them out of nearly all of the elements of the corporate governance system applicable to public companies—is not the only one that matters. In Europe, many regulations relating to disclosure and governance are not limited to public companies. Private equity firms that operate in Europe have to be mindful of European Union regulations regarding diversity and other social concerns. For example, the EU's Sustainable Finance Disclosure Regulation may force private equity firms to keep track of board gender diversity and pay gaps. Particularly in Europe, the private equity industry has at times also attempted to develop forms of self-regulation on a range of issues, "clearly aimed at forestalling the threat of mandatory intervention." Many private equity funds have been out in front of public companies in making statements about sustainability. Both Carlyle and KKR started voluntarily publishing sustainability reports, with disclosure of the kind that the SEC is now considering requiring of public companies.

In September 2021, Carlyle and Blackstone joined with some of their larger institutional investors, including the California Public Employees' Retirement System, to share information about emissions, diversity, and the treatment of employees across companies. Because many private equity funds raise money from pension and sovereign wealth funds, which are increasingly focused on topics such as climate change and inequality, some of them have rebranded themselves as ESG funds. A recent *Harvard Business Review* column noted that "90% of [surveyed private equity investors] factor ESG into

124 their investment decisions and 77% use it as a criterion in selecting general partners."

The Threat of Politics to Index Funds and Private Equity Funds

For index funds, the political threats are clear and pointed. Red state politicians are beginning to impose their own legal requirements as a condition of doing business. Prompted by the coal industry, "West Virginia's treasury investment board [in 2022] stopped using a BlackRock fund after the money manager urged companies to achieve net-zero emissions by 2050." A letter sent to BlackRock in August 2022 by nineteen Republican attorneys general, led by officials from states with significant oil and gas industry activity, accused the firm of prioritizing its climate agenda over pensioners' investments, and of antitrust violations in pursuing net zero commitments in concert with other investors. The state treasurers of West Virginia, Louisiana, and Arkansas pulled $700 million out of BlackRock funds because they consider the firm to be too focused on environmental issues. Ron DeSantis, governor of a state with 8,000 miles of low-lying coastland, banned state pension funds from screening for climate and other ESG risks.

At the federal level, a Republican-sponsored bill pending in the Senate would remove index funds' governance power altogether, transferring it to corporate boards and to other institutional investors. Senate Bill 4241 would require large index funds to pass through votes on non-routine matters to fund shareholders, or (at the fund sponsors' option) not vote at all. The costs involved in pass-throughs are so large as to make non-voting by the funds inevitable: the bill is designed simply to take index funds out of corporate governance and the political world altogether.

Index funds and the broader ESG movement have figured in the kinds of speechifying and writing that politicians use to raise funds and build popular support. Mike Pence was an early attacker of "woke capitalism," a neologism with its own Wikipedia entry attributing the term to conservative *New York Times* columnist Ross Douthat. ESG, Pence wrote in the *Wall Street Journal*, is a "pernicious strategy" of "an unelected cabal of bureaucrats" and "large and powerful Wall Street financiers." Pence's article was pure show. His solution—the "next Republican president and GOP Congress should work to end the use of ESG principles nationwide"—would violate the First Amendment and override investment decisionmaking across the entire financial sector. But as virtue signaling, it was no doubt useful in helping him connect to some in his party's base.

Glenn Beck labeled a radio show "Why are woke CEOs using ESG to DESTROY our free market?" (The capital letters are his.) Senator Tom Cotton has publicly demanded answers from BlackRock about its involvement with an environmental activist organization, Climate Action 100+, threatening an antitrust action of some kind in retaliation.

Of course, as puffed up and extreme as some of these claims are, the political threats they represent are aspects of a reality: the problem of twelve. As Charlie Munger, Warren Buffett's longtime partner, pungently put it: "We have a new bunch of emperors, and they're the people who vote the shares in the index funds. I think the world of Larry Fink, but I'm not sure I want him to be my emperor."

126   If it were not for the giant scale of the index funds, and their consequent political power, the political attacks on them would not be occurring. For index funds, the problem of twelve is already manifest in the political sphere.

Threats to private equity funds so far have had a different character. They mostly come from the left and from Democratic politicians and officials. Private equity groups have been called "locusts," "asset strippers," "casino capitalists," and "predators." Private equity funds' tax advantages are in the crosshairs of some members of the Democratic leadership, and the largest private equity funds are facing increasing demands for information from public pension funds, particularly in blue states. Commentators attack private equity on an investment basis, too, arguing they do not in fact produce better risk-adjusted returns.

In 2014, Andrew Bowden, who was head of the SEC's Divisions of Examinations at the time, made it clear in a highly publicized speech that the SEC had begun focusing on the private equity industry. Enforcement actions followed. Similar public messaging from the SEC followed in 2015 and 2016. More recently, the SEC has proposed requiring disclosure by private equity funds. The proposal continues a trend of increasing public disclosure obligations on private funds. Three Democratic US senators have introduced a bill that would require public reporting by any company above a set size, regardless of its number of shareholders or whether it is listed on a stock exchange, which would impose transparency on the largest companies owned by private equity funds.

A broader attack renews concerns dating back to the 1980s—that private equity buyouts produce excessive debt, a

thinning out of the US economy, conflicts of interest, and the
illegitimate use of insider information. The focus of this threat
is the potential negative effects of buyouts on acquired companies, or on the banks that fund buyouts. Three separate bills
were pending in 2019 aimed at the industry, including H.R.3848,
the "Stop Wall Street Looting Act" (reintroduced in 2021),
backed by five senators and led by Elizabeth Warren. That bill
would:

- Require private equity firms (not simply private equity
  funds) and their individual owners to "share responsibility for . . . liabilities of [portfolio] companies under their
  control—including debt, legal judgments and pension-
  related obligations;"
- Ban dividends to investors and the outsourcing of jobs for
  two years after a buyout;
- Prioritize worker pay in the bankruptcy process;
- End the immunity of private equity firms from liability
  when portfolio companies break the law, including the
  WARN Act (required before mass layoffs);
- Require private equity managers to disclose fees, returns,
  and other information; and
- Reinstate Dodd-Frank provisions requiring financial companies that arrange corporate debt securitization to retain
  risk.

Democrats have questioned a British company's plan to
sell its baby formula unit to a buyout fund, based on concerns
that this could shallow out a market segment already gripped
by critical shortages. Antitrust concerns overlap with these

128   broader attacks. The Biden administration is reportedly taking on private equity, with a focus on the antitrust effects of roll-ups in specific sectors, such as hospitals and data centers.

The policy merits of enhanced regulation of private equity in any of these ways are debatable. The political risks to the industry are not. As with index funds, scale and power attracts attention from other political actors. The private equity industry's problem of twelve is already manifest in US politics.

What Can Be Done?

What can be done about the problem of twelve that index funds and private equity funds create? Can we solve the problem? If not, can we manage it? Can we reduce the political and policy risks that each type of financial institution creates and faces, without reducing the economic benefits they create?

These funds' benefits are important to keep in mind as we consider proposals for policy changes to address the problem of twelve. Both types of funds perform financial functions, and are part of the dynamism and growth of the global economy. Any policy response to the problem of twelve should acknowledge and attempt to preserve capitalism's benefits.

Simple "solutions" to the problem of twelve—caps, bans, or complicated laws that assume individual investors can or will be willing to control the funds—are likely to be mistakes, and are unlikely to attract bipartisan support. Indeed, the size of the benefits of index funds, and the reasons that so much capital is currently managed by private equity funds, mean that the problem of twelve is better thought of not as a problem to be

130   solved, but as a dilemma to be managed. In some ways, the problem of twelve is a double problem: it's the threat posed by funds, and also the political risk posed by threats to funds. American history has produced episodes in which the political response to the growth of financial institutions was likely an overreaction, rather than an improvement. Any policy interventions should be cautious and provisional, and involve the delegation of authority to expert regulatory agencies, giving them the ability to adjust and refine how the law applies over time, as markets respond and evolve.

The core proposals advanced here involve greater transparency, or disclosure, and adaptations of the legal requirements of public consultation that currently apply to government agencies. For index funds, which already are playing a quasi-regulatory role over public companies, these tools should make intuitive sense. For private equity funds, which are designed to evade disclosure laws, the match is less good, but transparency and public consultation may be adaptable to the private equity business model. Because of the difficulties associated with major new legislation in our current political moment, both industries would be wise to embrace stronger forms of binding self-regulation.

Let us briefly review the benefits of index funds and private equity funds before we consider what might be done to address the problems of twelve that they create.

Index funds produce huge gains for middle-class investors relative to the alternatives. The benefits of index funds are clear, large, and both direct and indirect. Directly, they have allowed millions of Americans to diversify their investments safely at a low cost. Indirectly, they have increased competitive pressure on asset management generally. Index funds also likely have had positive effects in helping control the inclinations of managers of public companies to pursue pet projects, overcompensate themselves, or otherwise deviate from what the owners of the companies would want.

What about private equity funds? One immediate question is that, if the reason that index funds have succeeded is that the market is just really hard to beat, why doesn't the same logic apply to private equity funds? Why shouldn't we see index funds as just as big a conceptual challenge to private equity funds as they are to actively managed funds investing in public companies?

The research on private equity funds' benefits is much more tentative and contested than it is for index funds. Many industry voices loudly proclaim that private equity generates superior returns, but these claims are often based on raw return data—that is, unadjusted for risk and not benchmarked against alternatives—or they rely on private and unverified data. Even unadjusted raw return data show a decline over time in private equity's ability to generate value for investors. Other studies find that, appropriately benchmarked, private equity matches but does not beat the market—which, given the significant fees private equity firms charge, implies that they underperform for investors.

Part of the difficulty of determining whether private equity firms add value is precisely that they are private: it is hard to get data on their performance, so, compared to index funds, relatively few researchers have attempted to examine their investment performance rigorously, and those few attempts remain tentative and hard to replicate or validate. As a result, no general

132　consensus exists that private equity is currently adding value for even its own investors overall, much less for society as a whole. Yet large institutions continue to invest in private equity funds.

Having laid out a summary of the massive benefits of index funds, and the potential but uncertain benefits of private equity funds, it remains to specify the "problem of twelve" a little more precisely. To believe the problem exists, it is enough to review the persistence of similar issues throughout US history, and to understand the way in which the two types of funds are already heavily engaged in politics, and are coming under new political threats. But to try to manage the problem, we need a more refined diagnosis. The three core elements of that diagnosis are that the size and potential influence of index and private equity funds was accidental—unplanned—and not really part of their core financial function; that both types of funds operate in or use their power to lobby to expand or preserve regulatory gaps; and that there is a lack of transparency about what these funds are doing with their wealth and power.

Index funds' success has produced legitimacy and accountability deficits, which stem from their origin as accidental powers, and from regulatory gaps, also owing to their unplanned rise to influence. One key element of the regulatory gap is a lack of transparency on how they use their power. Private equity funds and the firms that sponsor and control them also face legitimacy and accountability deficits, which derive from unintended consequences of the private and public decisions that created the funds and from the unexpected success they have had in expanding their size and role. It seems clear that no one

would have imagined in watching the early buyouts of the 1970s
that one day the industry would oversee one in nine jobs in the
US private sector economy.

Private equity's legitimacy deficit primarily derives from
its privacy—or, to use another word, its secrecy. Compared to
the index fund industry, it discloses far less even to its investors, much less to the public. In the mid-2000s, amid a massive
buyout wave, the industry's own perceived need for more transparency was one reason for it to form its first formal trade group.
"The public wants to know who is buying up corporate America,"
said Felix G. Rohatyn, a longtime leader of Wall Street's investment banking industry. "It will be interesting to see how far
those at the top are willing to pull back the veil." Not very far, as
it turned out. The trade group remained quite modest in scope
for many years. Even today, more information about private
equity comes from its investors than from the firms that make
up the industry.

The accountability deficit for private equity funds is also
deeper than it is for index funds. The presumption is that investors in private equity funds are either wealthy individuals or
institutions like pension funds, endowments, and sovereign
funds, so they can take care of themselves. But the institutions
themselves are acting on behalf of dispersed individuals, who
are not in a position to make any demands. The limited disclosures now required of private equity firms stem from the
Dodd-Frank Act, which only addressed one dimension of private equity conduct—the potential for systemic risk.

Individual beneficiaries of pension funds that invest in private equity funds do not typically know about, much less require

134   their pension fund agents to demand from private equity advisors, the kinds of accountability that would normally accompany significant financial power. Not only are private equity funds not governed by mechanisms of voting accountability, they only face whatever accountability mechanisms the institutional investor agents who supply them with capital demand. Their incentives to seek information to hold the funds to account for their overall risk-taking and for their social impacts are weak at best.

Another way of putting the point is to say that private equity funds are not fully private. "Private" implies an individual owner, or a small number of individual owners, who are entitled to bind themselves and their property through contract. But over the years, private equity funds have successfully lobbied for legal permission to raise capital from thousands of dispersed investors without triggering SEC registration and the governance and disclosure requirements that apply to public companies.

Most capital invested through private equity is not invested on behalf of wealthy individuals, who might be presumed to be able to look after themselves. Instead, private equity's capital is now mostly raised from other institutions, who manage money on behalf of thousands of economic beneficiaries, adding up to more than 20 million people. Other institutional investors in private equity funds—university endowments, insurance companies, and sovereign funds—also invest on behalf of large numbers of people, representing millions of investors in the aggregate. Only in a strictly formal sense do private equity funds invest private money. Few of the ultimate beneficiaries of private equity investments—retirees, insured people, public school teachers, fund investors, citizens of countries with sovereign funds—are even aware that their labor and the compensation attached to it is being invested by KKR or Blackstone. Private equity funds do not give any information directly to end-beneficiaries about how their capital is being used, and end-beneficiaries do not have any effective way to monitor the agents who negotiate investments in private equity funds. They do not disclose to end-beneficiaries the names, fees, governance arrangements, or conflict-of-interest protections that they negotiate with private equity firms. The primary way in which private equity is private is that its business is clothed in secrecy.

Finally, private equity funds lock in their investors for five years or longer, dramatically limiting the exit option in governance. Institutional investors' own end-beneficiaries typically have no ability to withdraw money invested in private equity funds. Reputation or experience with older funds sponsored by the same private equity advisor no doubt informs whether institutions invest in new funds. But the time lag provides only weak accountability relative to current exit rights, as provided to investors in public companies and index funds, and is greatly impaired given the very limited disclosures such funds currently make, even after a fund is liquidated.

Plausible Policy Options

Having specified the nature of the problem of twelve as consisting in large part of accountability and legitimacy deficits arising from unintended consequences of past regulatory and private investment decisions, we now turn to the question of what to do. I will lay out several cautious approaches for both

136   types of funds, and then consider bolder options that have
        already been proposed by others. Readers should not expect
        simple solutions. What we are likely to develop is a least-bad
        set of policy responses that reduce, without eliminating, the
        problem of twelve, while preserving the benefits these funds can
        create.

        Disclosure has promise as a partial response to the problem
        of twelve. While it is not a solution to the problem of twelve,
        disclosure is more powerful than it may seem. Additional dis-
        closure mandates will be stoutly resisted at every step by both
        the index fund and private equity industries. Indeed, limiting
        disclosure is one of the key elements of the private equity busi-
        ness model. One reason for that resistance is that more trans-
        parency will reveal to a greater extent how important these
        institutions have already become.

        The SEC should require index funds to report their portfolio
        company voting on a more frequent basis than currently (the
        requirement is only annual). Several large fund complexes are
        voluntarily reporting quarterly. A faster cadence of after-the-fact
        electronic vote reporting is now cheaper than in the past, and
        would not impose undue costs on fund investors. The SEC may
        have been reluctant to speed up reporting, because for smaller
        advisory companies the compliance burden might outweigh the
        cost. But the SEC's habit of regulating the entire mutual fund
        industry identically is not a requirement under the Investment
        Company Act. It is simply a habit, born of legal inertia. A rule
        tailored to the unique governance role that the very largest com-
        plexes play would not be unauthorized, and it would be in
        keeping with size-based tailoring Congress has authorized and

that the SEC has used in other areas of regulation. There is some value in applying this more broadly, beyond just index funds. Some actively managed funds also have significant voting power over some public companies. Frequent voting disclosures could apply to any advisor with sufficient assets under management as to provide significant voting power (for example, control of more than 1 percent of the shares) in a company.

More ambitiously, the SEC could also require fund advisors to disclose in more detail how they go about fulfilling their fiduciary obligations to vote fund shares. Advisors could provide better qualitative disclosures about how they develop voting positions on new issues as they emerge. Currently, the only time that fund investors learn about a fund advisor's inclinations on a given policy issue is after the advisor has voted on proposals. It would be better to inform fund investors beforehand, so they would know that a new kind of governance issue has arisen, and that the fund advisor is considering how to respond. Some issues are too company-specific for advance disclosure to be feasible, but often issues arise at one company and then become the subject of votes at multiple companies over time. If advisors were to identify emerging issues proactively for their own fund shareholders, the shareholders would be better able to respond—for example by selling fund shares—based on how the advisor plans to respond to the issue.

New disclosures of this type could include descriptions of:

- Any procedures they use to develop standing voting positions on topics that recur in voting on shareholder proposals or other kinds of votes

- How they choose which companies with which to engage, and how they do so
- What engagements they have completed, and what topics were discussed with company management
- Whether they have any internal policies on who performs those engagements
- From whom they seek advice when developing voting positions
- What conflict of interest policies and procedures on voting they have and how they are enforced
- Whether and why they vote identically across the funds in a complex, or differently in different situations

Such disclosures could be regularly updated, and could be linked to voting disclosures in a way that better allows fund investors to understand how and why the voting power derived from their investments is being used as it is. Such disclosures should flag emerging issues—shareholder proposals that are materially different from prior proposals—before the fund advisor has settled on a voting position.

Disclosure would also address private equity's legitimacy and accountability deficits. This would be far more problematic for private equity than it is for index funds, because their business model is built around maintaining secrecy. Even the modest new reporting requirements the SEC proposed in 2022 have encountered fierce resistance. Any bolder reform, one that would impose on private equity–owned companies a full SEC reporting regime, is likely to be viewed as an existential threat by the industry. Disclosures that would be viewed as tolerable are likely to be significantly narrower, shallower, and

less frequent than the full set of disclosures required of public
companies. This suggests a need to think beyond disclosure to
more substantive regulations.

Beyond disclosure requirements, advisors could be required
to engage regularly with their investors in some structured way.
This could be done through online discussion forums, by creating investor-specific portals, by posting possible voting positions on new topics for investor comment, or by some other
means. In effect, the very largest complexes could be required to
engage in a process designed to allow their very dispersed investors to provide input to the advisors in their decisionmaking.
For the pension funds and mutual funds that invest in private
equity, this could also be done at the fund level. That is, private
equity funds could be required to engage with their institutional investors, and pension and other funds could be required
to report to and engage with their own investors about those
fund-level engagements.

Such consultative requirements could be written so as to
not bind the fund advisor to public input; it need not be a
pass-through of votes or authority, which would likely not be
used widely enough to be effective. Instead, consultations
would be a way for interested and engaged end-investors to provide information about their views on the topics on which index
funds vote, and about how private equity funds make decisions.
For example, funds of either type might ask their investors for
their overall views on topics such as climate, working conditions, or large-scale layoffs. Index funds might give their own
investors the ability to set voting guidelines, or to rely on guidelines provided by third parties.

140   One may be skeptical about the value of such a process. If only the process but not the results are binding, what is the point? But for many years, we have required similar behavior of regulatory agencies. Courts do not (or at least should not) overturn regulations that they think are unwise or poor policy; they do overturn regulations if the agencies involved failed to let the public have an opportunity to comment on them before being adopted.

Perhaps that's only for show, too. But a less cynical view is that even if it is rare that a public comment to a regulatory agency provides genuinely new, true, and important information or insight into a policy question, they sometimes do that, and the act of providing the information can be valuable to those providing it. Public comments commonly result in proposed rules being formally withdrawn, abandoned, or significantly revised. A public engagement process can allow for some new information to be shared in a decision-timely way.

Meanwhile, the option to participate in a process of decisionmaking mitigates the risks associated with all-or-nothing decisions by individuals controlling large amounts of power or wealth, like the managers of index funds and private equity funds. Is this a solution to the problem of twelve? No. But it would be better than doing nothing about the problem, and better than simply destroying or imposing large new costs on the funds, as some proposed policy reforms (such as pass-through voting) would do.

Conclusion

Two types of financial institutions that emerged in the second half of the twentieth century—index funds and private equity funds—have grown faster than the economy overall, and have become powerful forces in the economy and in the political system. Their success has created a new problem of twelve: as with central banks, money trusts, and insurance companies before them, these funds have become threats to American-style democratically managed capitalism. Index fund success is built on real and important economic benefits they generate for ordinary investors. Private equity's benefits to society are less clear, but they, too, continue to attract investment on behalf of ordinary retirees and workers, through pension funds.

It is tempting, perhaps intrinsically human, to want to view any new phenomenon as either being "good" or "bad," and to respond accordingly. But often neither extreme position is true. In hindsight, the US political system's killing of the First and Second Banks of the United States was a mistake. Central banks are socially useful as well as dangerous. The Federal Reserve

142   Board, which eventually replaced them, is a mixed public/private body that operates within American democratic traditions and still provides an effective (if always controversial) means to manage the money supply. Such a mixed body is a better way to manage the problem of twelve that a central bank creates than either attempting to operate a modern economy without one, or letting such a potentially all-corrupting organization operate without checks and balances.

Index funds are both good and bad. Private equity funds are both good and bad. Indeed, capitalism itself is both good and bad. The title of this book notwithstanding, financial capitalism generally, and financial institutions such as index and private equity funds in particular, present not a "problem" if that implies a "solution" to be found, but a deep conflict between economics and politics, with the right response being persistent public (legal, regulatory, governmental, democratic, political) oversight and management of private activity. The deep conflict in finance happens because economies of scale are powerful, and produce massive social benefits, only by way of centralizing wealth in a few hands, which then creates a real threat to democracy. History contains many examples of ways to manage these dilemmas, rather than do nothing or kill the institutions creating the dilemma: geographic fragmentation, functional separation, activity regulation, antitrust, disclosure, procedural requirements, mixed public/private governance, stronger enforcement of anti-influence laws.

The analogy of the Fed is also a useful caution about thinking of antitrust as the sole solution to the problem of twelve created by index and private equity funds. A truly fragmented central bank would be a contradiction in terms. A robust government armed with antitrust power can achieve much good in protecting against the threats (both economic and political) of big corporations (the original "trusts"). But some functions of the financial system require institutions that are concentrated and large. Greater antitrust management of index and private equity funds and the companies they own would likely be an improvement over the status quo, in ways suggested in this book.

But antitrust alone is not a solution to the problem of twelve. If fragmented to a non-threatening size, index funds could not deliver the same low-cost investment benefits of diversification. If rendered truly passive, such as by taking away their voting power, index funds would magnify the agency costs of public companies, and only bring back the problems Berle and Means identified a century ago. A clear trade-off exists between the benefits flowing from economies of scale, and the risks to political economy of scale and concentration. This trade-off calls for hybrid public/private organizations, which require more than antitrust as a response to size and power.

Greater requirements of mandated disclosure and governance were necessary to managing the problem of twelve created by a central bank, and they will be necessary to managing the problem of twelve created by index and private equity funds. To see the rough potential of disclosure and governance in responding to the funds, one need only note that disclosure and governance are the ways that index funds currently exert power. The same tools that allow index funds to have major influence over the US economy can be used to increase their legitimacy and accountability in doing so.

The importance of these tools is also clear from how the funds were built on regulatory avoidance—they have been

144   designed to sit outside traditional regulatory systems that
emerged in the New Deal. De- and re-regulatory choices since
the 1980s have enlarged spaces for massive amounts of dispersed investment capital to be invested with little public oversight. Private equity is almost entirely dark. Index funds are
more transparent than private equity funds, but exert power in
the regulatory gap between "control" (regulated) and "influence"
(not regulated).

Every generation or two, entrepreneurs create a new institution to capture economies of scale in finance. As the institution's size and power grows, it comes to threaten democracy
itself. How the political system responds to the threat is an
important, quasi-constitutional choice. Extreme choices tend
to be bad ones: if gridlock blocks any response, the threat only
grows; if the political system kills or maims the institution, it
also destroys the benefits the institution produces. Better to
manage the threat with disclosure and public oversight, and to
not let the perfect be the enemy of the good. Good responses
to today's problem of twelve will not be a permanent resolution
of the tensions between democracy and capitalism, but they
will lay a foundation for future generations to manage tomor-
row's problem of twelve.

I thank my family (Ingrid, Ava, Oliver, and Henry) and the late John Bogle for helping ground this project in good conversations and curiosity. For comments and discussions, I also thank William Birdthistle, Sean Collins, Einer Elhauge, George Georgiev, Eric Goodwin, Jeff Gordon, Caleb Griffin, Robin Greenwood, Howell Jackson, Nicholas Lemann, Dorothy Lund, Mark Roe, Hal Scott, Suraj Srinivasan, Dan Tarullo, and participants in workshops at Columbia Law School, University of Connecticut Law School, Georgetown University Law Center, The Wharton School, University of Virginia, University of Arkansas School of Law, the Program on International Financial Systems, and Harvard Law School for helpful comments on the paper on which this book was partly based. I benefited from research assistance from Chaim Herbstman and Larson Ishii. I also benefited from conversations with individuals at or formerly at the "Big Four" index funds, congressional staff, and staff and commissioners of the Securities and Exchange Commission. Stace Tollman provided excellent assistance throughout, and Jimmy So and Leigh Grossman provided helpful editing support for the book. All errors remain my responsibility.

CHAPTER ONE

Adolf A. Berle and Gardiner C. Means, *The Modern Corporation and Private Property* (1932)

Eric A. Posner and E. Glen Weyl, *Radical Markets: Uprooting Capitalism and Democracy for a Just Society* (2019)

Mark J. Roe, Strong Managers, *Weak Owners: The Political Roots of American Corporate Finance* (1994)

CHAPTER TWO

John Bogle, *The First Index Mutual Fund: A History of Vanguard Index Trust and the Vanguard Index Strategy* (2006)

John C. Coates and R. Glenn Hubbard, "Competition in the Mutual Fund Industry: Evidence and Implications for Policy," 33 *Journal of Corporation Law* 151 (2008)

Dorothy Shapiro Lund, The Case Against Passive Shareholder Voting, 43 *Journal of Corporation Law* 493 (2018)

Adriana Z. Robertson, Passive in Name Only: Delegated Management and "Index" Investing, 36 *Yale Journal on Regulation* 795 (2019)

CHAPTER THREE

William A. Birdthistle and M. Todd Henderson, One Hat Too Many? Investment Desegregation in Private Equity, 76 *University of Chicago Law Review* 45 (2009)

Steven J. Davis, John Haltiwanger, Kyle Handley, Ron Jarmin, Josh Lerner, and Javier Miranda, "Private Equity, Jobs, and Productivity," 104:12 *American Economic Review* 3956-90 (2014)

Elisabeth de Fontenay, "The Deregulation of Private Capital and the Decline of the Public Company," 68 *Hastings Law Journal* 445 (2017)

Elisabeth de Fontenay, "Private Equity's Governance Advantage: 147
A Requiem," 99 *Boston University Law Review* 1095-1122 (2019)

Steven N. Kaplan & Per Strömberg, "Leveraged Buyouts and Private Equity,"
23 *Journal of Economic Perspectives* 121 (2009)

CHAPTER FOUR

William W. Clayton, Public Investors, Private Funds, and State Law, 72
Baylor Law Review 294 (2020)

Gerald F. Davis and Tracy A. Thompson, A Social Movement Perspective on
Corporate Control, 39 *Administrative Science Quarterly* 141-73 (Mar. 1994)

Martin C. Schmalz, "Recent Studies on Common Ownership, Firm
Behavior, and Market Outcomes," 66 *Antitrust Bulletin* 12 (2021)

Roberto Tallarita, "Stockholder Politics," 73:6 *Hastings Law Journal* 1617
(2022)

CHAPTER FIVE

Catherine R. Albiston and Catherine L. Fisk, "Precarious Work and
Precarious Welfare: How the Pandemic Reveals Fundamental Flaws of the
U.S. Social Safety Net," 42 *Berkeley Journal of Employment and Labor Law* 257
(2021)

Heitor Almeida and Thomas Philippon, "The Risk-Adjusted Cost of
Financial Distress," 62:6 *The Journal of Finance* 2557-2586 (2007)

Edith S Hotchkiss, David C Smith, Per Strömberg, Private Equity and the
Resolution of Financial Distress. 10:4 *Review of Corporate Finance Studies*
694-747 (2021)

NOTES

INTRODUCTION

13   magnifies the gales of "creative destruction": Joseph A. Schumpeter, *Capitalism, Socialism and Democracy* (1942).

13   a democratic republic built on Montesquieu's separation of powers: *De L'esprit Des Lois* (1748). Donald Lutz famously argued Montesquieu had more influence in British North America prior to the American Revolution than any other European thinker. Donald S. Lutz, "The Relative Influence of European Writers on Late Eighteenth-Century American Political Thought," *Am. Pol. Sci. Rev.* 78:1 (1984), 189–97.

13   created by central banks, private banks, insurance companies, and "money trusts": Mark J. Roe, *Strong Managers, Weak Owners: The Political Roots of American Corporate Finance* (1994).

CHAPTER ONE

17   has for over a hundred years consisted of public companies' shares: John C. Coates, "Thirty Years of Evolution in the Roles of Institutional Investors in Corporate Governance," in *Research Handbook on Shareholder Power* (Jennifer Hill and Randall Thomas, eds., Edward Elgar, 2015), summarizing data since 1980 from the Federal Reserve.

000   the creation and governance of public companies: Much of this story owes a first-order debt to Mark J. Roe, *Strong Managers, Weak Owners: The Political Roots of American Corporate Finance* (1994).

18   these features also characterize major financial institutions: Mark J. Roe, *Strong Managers, Weak Owners: The Political Roots of American Corporate Finance* (1994); Morton Keller, *The Life Insurance Enterprise, 1885–1910—A Study in the Limits of Corporate Power* (1963); The "Money Trust," *New York Times*, July 24, 1911.

19   what Henry Luce called "the American Century": Henry Luce, "The American Century," *Life*, February 17, 1941.

20   serving neither social ends nor the private interests of their shareholders: Adolf A. Berle and Gardiner C. Means, *The Modern Corporation and Private Property* (1932).

21   both at the time and since: Brian Cheffins has noted that Berle and Means only identified eighty-eight of the two hundred companies they analyzed as having true separation of ownership and control, with the majority remaining under control of one or more dominant shareholders. "The Rise and Fall (?) of the Berle-Means Corporation," *Seattle U. L. Rev.* 42 (2019), 445, 450 n.20. Cheffins also notes, however, that the trend toward dispersed ownership was well underway in 1932, and that by 1970, their diagnosis was generally complete (p. 454); see also Robert A. Dahl, *After the Revolution* (1970), 104. ("Every literate person now rightly takes for granted what Berle and Means established four decades ago in their famous study.")

21　**decades of muckraking journalistic attacks:** See, for instance, Ida M. Tarbell, "The History of Standard Oil," *McClure's Magazine*, November 1902.

21　**the best disinfectant for the resulting ills of corruption and waste:** Louis Brandeis, *Other People's Money and How the Bankers Use It* (New York: Stokes, 1914). ("Publicity is justly commended as a remedy for social and industrial diseases. Sunlight is said to be the best of disinfectants; electric light the most efficient policeman."); see also Thomas K. McCraw, *Prophets of Regulation* (Harvard University Press, 1984), discussing Brandeis and his critique of big companies.

21　**"[w]ithin ten weeks of the . . . crash":** Joel Seligman, *The Transformation of Wall Street*, 5.

22　**"there was obvious need to restore buyers' confidence":** Thomas K. McCraw, *Prophets of Regulation*, 168.

22　**revealed rampant corporate abuse:** Pecora Commission Report

1934, available at "Pecora Commission Report—Stock Exchange Practices Report 1934," Scribd.com, https://tinyurl.com /5n7j9yd8.

22　**"incomparably the greatest reach of power in private hands in our entire history":** Ron Chernow, *The House of Morgan: An American Banking Dynasty and the Rise of Modern Finance* (2001).

23　**who attacked them as "Russian":** See, for instance, "Stock Bill Fight to Open Today: Republicans Charge Fletcher-Rayburn Measure Move to Russianize Industry," *Wall Street Journal*, April 30, 1934, for attacks on securities law proposals.

23　**remained a live option in the US through World War II:** During this period, a majority of those polled supported public ownership of utilities, and nearly as many supported public ownership of banks as opposed it. Seymour Martin Lipset and William Schneider, *The Confidence Gap: Business, Labor, and Government in the Public Mind* (1987), 61; see also Robert S. McElvaine, *The Great Depression: America 1929–1941* (1984), 205. ("The Depression led many intellectuals into believing that some sort of social and ideological apocalypse was at hand . . . [and] scores of leading thinkers turned to Marx.") Former Delaware Chief Justice Leo Strine

150 has discussed the larger political context of the classic work by Berle and Means, in "Made for This Moment: The Enduring Relevance of Adolf Berle's Belief in a Global New Deal," working paper, May 17, 2018.

24 **"some form of socialism would be a good thing":** Lipset and Schneider, *The Confidence Gap*, note 17, at 283; see also McElvaine, *The Great Depression*, note 17, at 207 ("Nearly 60 percent of the poor questioned in a 1935 *Fortune* survey said that the government should not 'allow a man who has investments worth over a million dollars to keep them.'").

25 **No one investor would buy a controlling position:** John C. Coates and Suraj Srinivasan, *Corporate Governance, Core Reading* (Harvard Business Publishing, 2018), 11–12.

CHAPTER TWO

28 **fewer than half of attempts by outside shareholders to replace existing board members:** "Proxy Fights: 2020," Activist Insight (2020), 10, https://tinyurl.com /n3h9n7vk (reporting 168 out of 350 proxy contests succeeded in obtaining at least one board seat, either by settlement or after a vote).

29 **a sustainability executive from a petroleum refining and marketing company:** Robert G. Eccles and Colin Mayer, "Can a Tiny Hedge Fund Push ExxonMobil Towards Sustainability?" *Harvard Business Review*, January 20, 2021.

30 **in publications by MIT management professor Paul Cootner:** Paul Cootner, *The Random Character of Stock Market Prices* (1964). Even earlier, in 1960, two Chicago students conceived and wrote up a theoretical model for an "Unmanaged Investment Company," but this earlier work was not cited by later researchers or innovators. See Justin Fox, "Chapter 7: Jack Bogle Takes on the Performance Cult (and Wins)," in *The Myth of the Rational Market* (HarperCollins, 2011), 111–12.

30 **Princeton economist Burton G. Malkiel, Chicago economist Eugene Fama:** Burton G. Malkiel, *A Random Walk Down Wall Street* (1973), which drew on Burton G. Malkiel and Eugene F. Fama, "Efficient Capital Markets: A Review of Theory and Empirical Work," *Journal of Finance* 25, no. 2 (1970), 383–417.

30 **MIT economist Paul Samuelson:** Paul Samuelson, "Challenge to Judgement," *Journal of Portfolio Management* 1 (1974), 17–19.

30 **the still-standard model of how to price options on stock:** Fischer Black and Myron Scholes, "The Pricing of Options and Corporate Liabilities," *Journal of Political Economy* 81, no. 3 (1973),

637–54; Robert C. Merton (1973);
"Theory of Rational Option
Pricing," *Bell Journal of Economics
and Management Science* 4, no. 1
(The RAND Corporation, 1973),
141–83.

31 **the first index mutual fund
available to the general public:** An
earlier fund, Qualidex Fund, Inc.,
was privately organized in 1967 by
Richard A. Beach and filed a
registration statement with the
SEC on October 20, 1970, to
function "as an open-end,
diversified investment company
whose investment objective is to
approximate the performance of
the Dow Jones Industrial Stock
Average." The fund's registration
statement became effective on July
31, 1972. That fund, however, was
marketed to institutional investors,
and was not available to public
investors generally. The fund
eventually became included in the
Templeton Funds complex. Because
of John Templeton's aversion to the
index investing concept, the index
fund was liquidated in 1984.

31 **it would take funds invested
by its own investors:** Vanguard
also had another unusual feature:
its advisory company was owned
by the funds the advisory company
advised, and not by individuals or
other investors, making it
effectively a kind of "mutual,"
which blunted incentives for the
advisory firm managers to take
actions that would benefit the

advisory firm at the expense of
fund investors, such as
diversifying its operations.
Vanguard remains unique in having
this governance structure.

32 **People called the fund
"Bogle's Folly":** John Bogle, "The
First Index Mutual Fund: A History
of Vanguard Index Trust and the
Vanguard Index Strategy," Bogle
Financial Center, 2006.

33 **Many professionals can in
fact generate added value for their
investment clients:** Laurent
Barras, Olivier Scaillet, and Russ
Wermers, "False Discoveries in
Mutual Fund Performance:
Measuring Luck in Estimated
Alphas," *Journal of Finance* 65
(2010), 179–216 (75.4 percent of
funds have some skill); Jonathan
Berk and Jules van Binsbergen,
"Measuring Skill in the Mutual
Fund Industry," *Journal of Financial
Economics* 118 (2015), 1–20; K. J.
Martijn Cremers, Jon A. Fulkerson,
and Timothy B. Riley, "Challenging
the Conventional Wisdom on
Active Management: A Review of
the Past 20 Years of Academic
Literature on Actively Managed
Mutual Funds," *Fin. Anal. J.* 75
(2019), 1–28 (surveying studies).

33 **have gotten even lower over
time:** ICI Research Perspective
March 2021 // Vol. 27, No. 3, Trends
in the Expenses and Fees of Funds,
2020 ("Index equity mutual fund
expense ratios fell from 0.27

152   percent in 1996 to 0.06 percent in 2020.").

34   steadily but slowly increased their share of stock ownership: A new type of index fund—the exchange traded fund or ETF—was invented by State Street in 1992. SPDR Trust, Series 1, et al.; Notice of Application, ICA Release No. 18959 (September 17, 1992). For most governance purposes, and this essay, ETFs and indexed mutual funds are similar. See Coates, "Thirty Years of Evolution in the Roles of Institutional Investors in Corporate Governance."

35   "together accounted for 43 percent of assets in long-term funds": ICI Factbook 2022, p. 29.

36   They report their assets as a share of all global companies or all US companies, for example: For instance, see BlackRock, 2019 Investment Stewardship Annual Report (August 2019), p. 25 (figure depicting BlackRock's assets as a share of global, total equity market capitalization at 4.06 percent, and ownership of Big Three as "just over 10%," without noting that their ownership of S&P 500 companies is significantly higher, as shown by the Apple, IBM, and Conoco examples discussed below at text accompanying notes 34–36); see also ICI Investment Company Fact Book 2020, Figure 2.9, p. 40 (figure labeled "Index Fund Share of US Stock Market Is Small" includes

total US stock market capitalization in denominator, shows domestic equity index fund ownership at 15 percent).

36   Much of that ownership is indexed: "Worldwide Regulated Open-End Fund Assets and Flows, Fourth Quarter 2018," Investment Company Institute, release, March 27, 2019, https://www.ici.org /research/stats/worldwide.

38   gave trustees both permission and an incentive to invest: Robert H. Sitkoff and Max Schanzenbach, "Did Reform of Prudent Trust Investment Laws Change Trust Portfolio Allocation?" *J. L. & Econ.* 50 (2007), 681.

40   index funds enjoy economies of scale—more so than other types of funds: If there were any doubt on the question, BlackRock staff published an article in 2022 confirming the point. Shreya Adiraju, Dalia Blass, Samara Cohen, Ananth Madhavan, and Salim Ramji, "On the Benefits of Scale Economies in Asset Management," *J. Portfolio Mgt.* 48, no. 5 (2022), 1.

41   up from 19 percent in 2009: ICI Factbook 2018, p. 43 (reporting indexed mutual funds and ETFs held 13 percent of US public equities, while active funds and ETFs held 14 percent).

41   than any three single investors have ever previously

held: None of the large advisory firms limit themselves to just active or passive management. Even Vanguard sponsors active funds, and Fidelity, its longtime rival, which (historically) predominantly focused on active management, now not only also sponsors passive funds, but has seen its strongest growth in passives, such that it now could be legitimately viewed as a "Big Fourth" major index fund sponsor, in addition to the Big Three.

42 **The Big Four own more than 60 percent of the large:** John C. Coates, Ron Fein, Kevin Crenny, and L. Vivian Dong, "Quantifying Foreign Institutional Block Ownership at Publicly Traded U.S. Corporations," working paper, September 2016.

42 **a significant fraction of shareholders does not vote:** Individual shareholders typically vote only 28 percent of their 30 percent ownership of the S&P 500, and institutions other than the Big Three vote 70 percent of their 91 percent, compared to 100 percent voting by the Big Three. "2018 Proxy Season Review," ProxyPulse, October 2018, https://www .broadridge.com/proxypulse/ (reporting percentages for individuals and institutions overall); Fisch, Hamdani, & Solomon, "Passive Investors," working paper, June 29, 2018, p. 21 and note 111, http://ssrn.com

/abstract=3192069 (reporting percentage voted by Big Three). Given these data, the Big Three are already typically voting more than 27 percent of the total shares voted at S&P 500 firms.

42 **and the votes of other investors that follow the advice of proxy advisory firms:** See, for example, Stephen Choi, Jill Fisch, and Marcel Kahan, "The Power of Proxy Advisors: Myth or Reality?" 59 *Emory L. J.* 869 (2010), 905–6 (estimating impact of proxy advisory firms' voting recommendations on actual voting outcomes).

42 **will almost always include the median vote in such fights:** To be clear, the claim here is not that all index funds vote identically, or that they uniformly follow ISS or Glass Lewis's recommendations. They do not. See Ryan Bubb and Emiliano Catan, "The Party Structure of Mutual Funds," *Rev. Fin. Stud.* 35, no. 6 (2022), 2839–78 (showing that the large fund complexes tend to vote more deferentially to portfolio company managers than do other funds, particularly those who follow ISS or Glass Lewis's recommendations). Rather, the claims are that funds within a complex tend to vote uniformly, and a small group of index fund advisor managers control the voting of enough shares to determine the outcome of votes.

154

44   their legal obligations encourage some (arguably minimal) governance efforts: See, for instance, Department of Labor, Interpretive Bulletin Relating to the Exercise of Shareholder Rights and Written Statements of Investment Policy, including Proxy Voting Policies or Guidelines, available at https://www.dol.gov/sites/default /files/ebsa/2016-31515.pdf, the first iteration of which was issued in 1994, 59 Fed. Reg. 38863 (July 29, 1994). That policy reflected more informal guidance provided in a letter addressed to Helmuth Fandl, Chairman of the Retirement Board of Avon Products Inc., dated February 23, 1988, and a subsequent letter addressed to Robert A. G. Monks of Institutional Shareholder Services, Inc., dated January 23, 1990, which set forth the view that voting rights of portfolio company stock should be viewed as an asset of any benefit plan subject to the Employee Retirement Income Security Act of 1974; see also https://www.sec.gov/news/public -statement/statement-regarding -staff-proxy-advisory-letters (announcing repeal of no-action letters related to reliance on proxy advisory firms by investment advisors, arguably encouraging investment advisors to internalize governance activity).

44   some governance activity for public relations reasons: Marcel Kahan and Ed Rock, "Symbolic Corporate Governance Politics," 94 B.U. L. Rev. 1997 (2014).

46   what are sometimes derogatorily called "governistas": Theodore Mirvis, "Reflections on Airgas and Long-Term Value," Harvard Law School Forum on Corporate Governance and Financial Regulation, January 25, 2012, https://corpgov.law.harvard. edu/2012/01/25/reflections-on -airgas-and-long-term-value/.

46   the "governance machine": Dorothy Lund and Elizabeth Pollman, "The Corporate Governance Machine," *Colum. L. Rev.* 121 (2021), 2563.

46   it was BlackRock that pushed Exxon into disclosing the long-term portfolio impacts: See BlackRock's press release from May 31, 2017, https://www.blackrock .com/corporate/literature/press -release/blk-vote-bulletin-exxon -may-2017.pdf. This is not a criticism of BlackRock for its efforts in this area, which seem entirely aligned with shareholder and social value.

47   triggered a wave of media coverage: For instance, https:// www.washingtonpost.com/news /energy-environment/wp/2017/05 /31/exxonmobil-is-trying-to-fend -off-a-shareholder-rebellion-ove r-climate-change/ (*Washington Post* coverage); https://tinyurl.com /qnkkllr (*Wall Street Journal*

coverage); https://tinyurl.com
/r2fedg7 (Reuters coverage);
https://tinyurl.com/y822p58d (*New
York Times* coverage); https://
tinyurl.com/vxjuq7d (CNBC
coverage).

**47   had typically lagged
environmentally friendly trends:**
Eric Rosenbaum, "Exxon Mobil
Loses Support of a Powerful Voice
in Climate Change Policy," CNBC,
September 25, 2017, https://tinyurl
.com/ybo3gwru.

**47   in order to avoid losing
shareholder votes on the topic:** "In
2018, companies were more willing
to address proponent requests prior
to the general meeting, following
exceptionally high support levels in
2017, including majority support
levels at the high-profile meetings
of Exxon Mobil Corporation and
Occidental Petroleum
Corporation." "Climate Change and
Proxy Voting in the U.S. and
Europe," Harvard Law School Forum
on Corporate Governance, January
7, 2019, https://tinyurl.com
/qwcy6wh.

**47   "participated in over 2,000
engagements with nearly 1,500
companies":** "2019 Investment
Stewardship Annual Report,"
BlackRock, August 2019, p. 3.

**47   is a substantial increase from
2017:** "2019 Investment
Stewardship Annual Report,"
BlackRock, p. 24.

**48   Vanguard reported 868, up
from 443 in 2014:** "Vanguard
Investment Stewardship Report,"
2019, p. 36, https://tinyurl.com
/sd9qe4w; "State Street Global
Advisors Stewardship Report,"
2018–19, p. 3 https://tinyurl.com
/v663w3d.

**48   "responded to our call by
either adding a female director or
committing to do so":** "State
Street Global Advisors Stewardship
Report," 2018–19, note 54, p. 3.

**48   are typically pivotal if the top
index funds take similar
positions:** Dorothy Shapiro Lund,
"The Case Against Passive
Shareholder Voting," *Journal of
Corporation Law* 43 (2018), 493.

CHAPTER THREE

51   Private equity firms: An
important economic and legal
difference exists between the
"funds" that are the actual
economic owners of businesses,
and the "firms" that operate and
manage those funds. The difference
is explained below.

**51   one in nine private sector
workers:** "Economic Contribution
of the US Private Equity Sector in
2020," Ernst & Young, Prepared for
the American Investment Council,
May 2021.

**53   the rest of a private equity
fund's capital is raised primarily**

156   **from institutions:** In the SEC's latest report on private equity funds, pension plans owned 26 percent of large private equity funds, while individuals owned 6 percent. SEC Division of Investment Management, Private Funds Statistics, Fourth Calendar Quarter 2021 (July 19, 2022), p. 18. Other institutional investors in private equity funds include financial institutions, government and corporate pension plans, university endowments, foundations, sovereign wealth funds, funds of funds, and insurance companies. See also Rajesh Kumar, "Strategies of Banks and Other Financial Institutions," 2014, 243–54.

53   **so their deals were called "leveraged buyouts":** Steven N. Kaplan and Per Strömberg, "Leveraged Buyouts and Private Equity," *J. Econ. Persp.* 23 (2009), 121.

54   **the latter are heavily regulated:** See chapter two.

54   **Such asymmetric fees— "heads I win, tails you lose"—are illegal for index funds:** IAA Section 205. That section permits use by mutual funds of incentive fees only if they are symmetric above and below a specified index, known as "fulcrum fees." Section 205(b).

54   **their median holding period for a company is six years:** Kaplan and Strömberg, "Leveraged Buyouts and Private Equity," note 60.

55   **"gale of creative destruction":** Joseph A. Schumpeter, *Capitalism, Socialism and Democracy* (1942).

56   **managed assets that were 18 percent of total corporate equity:** These data are based on comparing data from the Federal Reserve Board's (Fed) Flow of Funds reports with private equity AUM from Preqin. Note that for private companies, Fed data are book values (or estimates), and may understate fair value. Hodak presents evidence that even as the number of US public companies fell by 40 percent from 1998 to 2013, the number of US private companies with $1 billion or more in revenues rose by 400 percent over that period. Mark Hodak, "The Growing Executive Compensation Advantage of Private Versus Public Companies," *J. Appl. Corp. Fin.* 26 (2014), 20–28.

56   **transitioning from the founding to a second generation:** John L. Chapman & Peter G. Klein, "Value Creation in Middle-Market Buyouts: A Transaction-Level Analysis," in Douglas Cumming, ed., *Private Equity: Fund Types, Risks and Returns, and Regulation* (2011), 229, 245–46.

57   **imposed a stricter review standard on management buyouts:** The SEC initially proposed to take a

role in reviewing the substantive fairness of such deals, after Delaware courts channeled fairness challenges into an appraisal remedy that was hamstrung by a financially backward framework for valuation by courts. But the SEC's proposal generated a political reaction, and the Delaware courts responded with more aggressive fairness review, both in appraisal cases and in fiduciary duty cases. The SEC instead adopted Rule 13e-3 in 1977, significantly increasing disclosure in management-led going private transactions. See generally John C. Coates, "'Fair Value' as a Default Rule of Corporate Law: Minority Discounts in Conflict Transactions," *U. Penn. L. Rev.* 147 (1999), 1251.

57 **the leverage in leveraged buyouts moved from the margins:** Starting in the 1950s, public companies—both operating, and with increasing frequency, publicly traded holding companies—borrowed funds to buy other public companies and restructure or sell off their often diversified assets. Warren Buffett (Berkshire Hathaway) and Victor Posner (DWG Corporation), Nelson Peltz (Trian), Saul Steinberg (Reliance Insurance), and Gerry Schwartz (Onex Corporation) all used this technique. Posner is sometimes credited with the phrase "leveraged buyout." R. Trehan, *The History of Leveraged Buyouts* (2006).

57 **legendarily wearing a coal-miner's headlamp:** Frederik Gieschen, "The Milken Way," Neckar Substack, September 27, 2021, https://tinyurl.com /yuxuxh38.

59 **a "breach of trust" with workers and communities:** Andrei Shleifer and Lawrence H Summers, "Breach of Trust in Hostile Takeovers," in Alan J Auerbach, ed., *Corporate Takeovers: Causes and Consequences* (1988), 33–56.

59 **predicted that public companies were the next dodo:** Michael C. Jensen, "Eclipse of the Public Corporation," *Harvard Business Review*, September– October, 1989.

59 **the most ever by a Wall Street firm:** Milken's salary of $295 million that year was also a record.

59 **the SEC opened an investigation:** James B. Stewart, *Den of Thieves* (1992); Daniel Fischel, *Payback: Conspiracy to Destroy Michael Milken and His Financial Revolution* (1996) (arguing prosecution of Milken was not justified, laws involved were too vague to be applied to Milken's conduct, and the prosecution was motivated by Wall Street banks who had lost profits to Drexel, labor unions whose employees had been laid off following buyouts, and a lawless political prosecutor, Rudolph Giuliani).

158

59 **Drexel plead guilty and agreed to a $650 million penalty:** *S.E.C. v. Drexel Burnham Lambert Inc.*, 837 F. Supp. 587 (S.D.N.Y. 1993).

59 **The junk bond market shut down:** See John C. Coates and Lawrence Lederman, "Management Buyouts and the Duties of Independent Directors to Shareholders and Creditors," in *Corporate Deleveragings and Restructurings* (Practising Law Institute, 1991); Sarah Bartlett, "United Airline Deal: A Costly Fiasco," *New York Times*, October 25, 1989.

60 **Kohlberg Kravis Roberts had sixty employees in 1989:** Michael C. Jensen, "Eclipse of the Public Corporation," *Harvard Business Review*, September–October 1989, 70.

60 **KKR today has thousands of employees, and hundreds of professionals:** KKR & Co. Inc., 2021 Form 10-K, p. 32, https://tinyurl .com/2p8n6ate (3,200 employees, 700 professionals).

60 **the public relations value of associating venture capital and private equity with small business:** This is illustrated by the very title of the 2012 "Jumpstart Our Business Start-ups Act," which included deregulatory changes that would only benefit large public companies. See also, e.g., Chairman Jay Clayton, Speech, Remarks on Capital Formation at the Nashville

36|86 Entrepreneurship Festival, August 29, 2018 (linking venture capital, small business, start-ups, and deregulation).

60 **Congress broadened the exemption in 1980:** The Small Business Investment Incentive Act of 1980.

60 **from an unlimited number of moderately wealthy accredited investors:** The SEC then (and now) defines so-called "accredited investors" as those with a net worth of $1 million and annual income of $200,000. When adopted, Reg D did not dramatically change the law for private equity or VC funds, who faced other regulations limiting their fundraising potential. But Reg D created the legal context for later lobbying to do just that.

60 **so did many businesses that could in no way be called small:** Another important regulatory change was the adoption in 1990 of Rule 144A, which permits securities to be resold without restriction to large institutional investors ("qualified institutional buyers" or "QIBs"). Again, at the time, this change did not primarily benefit private equity funds, since they were still governed by the ICA, which, as discussed in chapter two, strictly regulates mutual funds and other kinds of collective investments. In 1997, ordinary resales to any purchaser under Rule 144 were permitted after a

shortened, one-year waiting period, and in 2015, immediate resales to accredited investors were permitted.

61 relaxed its "prudent man" rule: "Thank You, ERISA, Thank You May Day . . .," *Forbes*, October 2, 1978; David Gumper, "Venture Capital Becoming More Widely Available," *Harvard Business Review* 57, January–February, 1979, 178–92. Further lobbying of the Department of Labor expanded and preserved the ability of VC (and later, private equity) funds to raise money freely from pension funds. See George W. Fenn, Nellie Liang, and Stephen Prowse, "The Economics of the Private Equity Market" Board of Governors of the Federal Reserve System, December 1995, 10–11, https://tinyurl.com/3fhsx5fr.

61 created a research and development tax credit: Pub. L. 97–34, title II, § 221(a), August 13, 1981, 95 Stat. 241, § 44F, now codified as amended at 26 U.S. Code § 41. For the examples, see https://tinyurl.com/yckxmu9j.

61 mandated federal agencies to set aside funding for businesses with fewer than five hundred employees: Josh Lerner, "The Government as Venture Capitalist: The Long-Run Impact of the SBIR Program," *J. Bus.* 72 (1999), 285.

61 biggest payoff from the political partnership: Testifying in favor of early versions of what

became NSMIA was Christopher W. Brody, Partner, Warburg Pincus & Company, on behalf of the NVCA. Securities Promotion Act of 1996: Hearing on S. 1815 Before the S. Comm. on Banking, Hous., and Urban Affairs, 104th Cong. 3–4, 6 (1996). Securities Investment Promotion Act of 1996 Report of the Committee on Banking, Housing, and Urban Affairs United States Senate to Accompany S. 1815, tinyurl.com/mrtfec3d, p. 2 ("Report on NSMIA"). Warburg Pincus was and is a top private equity firm.

61 a shift still underappreciated by many observers of the US capital markets: For useful context, see Elisabeth de Fontenay, "The Deregulation of Private Capital and the Decline of the Public Company," *Hastings Law Journal* 68 (2017), 445. For evidence of the importance of NSMIA, see Michael Ewens and Joan Farre-Mensa, "The Deregulation of the Private Equity Markets and the Decline in IPOs," *Rev. Fin. Stud.* 33 (2020), 5463–5509 (finding that after NSMIA's adoption late-stage start-ups are more likely to raise capital from out-of-state investors than early-stage start-ups, and late-stage start-ups' ability to raise large funding rounds increases more than for early-stage counterparts). For examples of commentators who overly stress regulation (such as in the Sarbanes-Oxley Act) and not the re-/ de-regulation in NSMIA as a cause of the decline of US IPOs, see "U.S. Public Equity Markets Are Stagnating," Committee on Capital Markets Regulation, April 2017, https://tinyurl.com/3efctnrr; "Rebuilding the IPO On-Ramp: Putting Emerging Companies and the Job Market Back to the Road on Growth," IPO Task Force, October 20, 2011, https://tinyurl.com /4fezr3n7. For evidence that overregulation of public companies is not a significant cause of any decline in US IPOs, see "SOX After Ten Years: A Multidisciplinary Review," *Accounting Horizons* 28, no. 3 (2014), 627.

62   that benefited financial interests at the expense of the public: The most egregious example of this was the deregulation of the derivatives industry, which contributed importantly to the financial crisis of 2008. Lynn A. Stout, "How Deregulating Derivatives Led to Disaster, and Why Re-Regulating Them Can Prevent Another," *Lombard Street* 1, no. 7 (July 2009), https://scholarship.law.cornell .edu/facpub/723.

62   let funds raise unlimited capital from unlimited numbers of institutions: NSMIA also (a) preempted state regulation of capital formation by companies relying on the key rule in Reg D, as well as by listed companies, which facilitates private equity funds (and other non-listed firms) to raise

capital across state lines without having to register as public companies or comply with multiple state laws, and (b) modified the securities laws overall, requiring the SEC (for the first time) to consider capital formation as a core goal, with investor protection. Seemingly commonsensical on its face, this change has been, in an era of increasing litigation over regulatory process, an increasingly important limit on the SEC's authority generally.

62   private funds were limited to a hundred investors: The ICA bars the kinds of high-powered incentive compensation VC and private equity fund advisors derive from their funds, and limits the use of leverage. It also requires frequent reporting of portfolio holdings.

62   could stay dark without any regulatory limit on their scale: Later lobbying by private fund trade groups further loosened Reg D. Congress adopted the JOBS Act in 2012, which repealed the long-standing ban on general advertising of securities offerings under Reg D. As a result, both companies and funds can publicly engage in fundraising without triggering SEC registration and disclosure requirements.

62   companies increasingly chose to delay or avoid altogether public listings: Elisabeth de Fontenay, "Private Equity's

Governance Advantage: A Requiem," *Boston University Law Review,* Vol. 99, No. 3, (2019).

63 **KKR proudly billed itself as a "buyout specialist":** Terry Dodsworth, "KKR Stirs Up Corporate Ownership with Leveraged Buyout Schemes," *Financial Times,* December 8, 1983, 23 ("buyout specialists like KKR").

63 **it pivoted to distressed investing, but continued to be identified as a buyout firm:** Suzanne Bowling, "KKR Acquiring Borden for RJR Stock," Associated Press, September 12, 1994.

63 **had spent $461 million to buy two hundred different publications:** Randall Smith, "KKR's K-III Investment Format Draws Mixed Reviews," *Wall Street Journal,* July 7, 1994.

63 **"buyout business has evolved into a private equity finance business":** Yvette Kantrow, "LBO Firms Turn to Leveraged Buildups," *Mergers & Acquisitions Rep.* 8, no. 23 (June 5, 1995), 3.

63 **KKR is now most frequently labeled simply as a private equity firm:** For instance, Alan Rappeport, et al, "Carried Interest Loophole Survives Another Political Battle," *New York Times,* August 5, 2022.

63 **it uses the word "buyout" precisely once:** KKR & Co. Inc.,

2021 Form 10-K, https://tinyurl .com/2p8n6ate.

64 **Perhaps unwittingly, so did the Federal Reserve Board:** George W. Fenn, Nellie Liang, and Stephen Prowse, "The Economics of the Private Equity Market."

64 **in fact, a portfolio company of a private equity fund has one shareholder:** Sometimes, private equity funds allow some investors to "co-invest," so the number of formal owners is greater than one, but it is still small.

64 **the economic beneficiaries of one private equity fund number in the thousands:** Analysis of data from https://publicplansdata .org/—a website developed and maintained by the Government Finance Officers Association (GFOA), MissionSquare Research Institute, the National Association of State Retirement Administrators, and the Center for Retirement Research at Boston College—shows that in 2020, 219 public pension plans had more than 50,000 beneficiaries each, and more than 14,000 for the median plan, totaling more than 10 million individual beneficiaries. Analysis of data from the Department of Labor for 2019 on private pension plans shows the 7,284 defined benefit plans with more than 100 participants had more than 7,280 participants each, with more than 12 million individuals participating

162   in all DB plans. Sovereign funds represent whole countries. Norway has a population of over 5 million; Kuwait has a population of over 4 million. Insurance companies have thousands or even millions of customers, whose capital is invested in private equity. Berkshire Hathaway's Geico reports over 17 million policyholders, https://tinyurl.com/47w6fuzx.

65 **had roughly $770 billion of global assets under management:** "Assets under management" for private equity funds include committed capital ("dry powder" in Wall Street jargon) as well as capital already deployed.

65 **had amassed global assets of $12.1 trillion:** Preqin.

65 **bank fees from private equity outstripped the fees:** Julian Evans, "The Return of Main Street Clients; Non-Financial Companies Have Broken Back into the List of the World's Best Investment Banking Clients After Several Years' Absence," *Financial News* (London), June 21, 2011.

67 **with high-profile private equity deal failures and bankruptcies:** Steven Davidoff Solomon, *Gods at War: Shotgun Takeovers, Government by Deal, and the Private Equity Implosion* (2009).

67 **the $10 billion in fees paid by private equity:** Liz Moyer, "Global Finance-Deals & Dealmakers: Credit Suisse Tops Goldman in Private Equity Fee Race," *Wall Street Journal*, January 5, 2011.

67 **was 40 times bigger than in private equity:** Josh Lerner and Paul Gompers, *Venture Capital and Private Equity: A Casebook* (1997).

68 **private equity firms announced a record $1.2 trillion worth of deals:** Stefania Palma and James Fontanella-Khan, "U.S. Trustbusters: Why Joe Biden Is Taking on Private Equity," *Financial Times*, August 22, 2022.

68 **private equity did 25 percent of all mergers and acquisitions:** Stefania Palma and James Fontanella-Khan, "U.S. Trustbusters: Why Joe Biden Is Taking on Private Equity."

68 **is far less sensitive to macroeconomic and financial fluctuations:** Vojislav Maksimovic, Gordon Phillips, and Liu Yang, "Private and Public Merger Waves," *J. Fin.* 68, no. 5 (2013), 2177; Jared Harford, "What Drives Merger Waves?" *J. Fin. Econ.* 77 (2005), 529–60.

69 **bulk of the industry's assets are accumulating within the largest private equity fund complexes:** In 2013, the SEC reported private equity funds advised by "large" advisors (those overseeing at least $2 billion in AUM) controlled two-thirds of all

private equity fund assets. Today the portion controlled by the largest private equity complexes is nearly 80 percent. The average—which reflects the ever-growing size of the largest funds—is seven to eight times larger than the median. Funds at the ninetieth percentile of the distribution have an average of $1.6 billion (gross) and $1.5 billion (net) each.

71 **more than 40 percent of US buyouts were club deals:** Kevin Dowd, "The Biggest Firms in Private Equity Are Clubbing Up Once Again," *Forbes*, May 9, 2021.

71 **Goldman Sachs:** Goldman, a multiservice global bank, then and now operates affiliated private equity operations.

72 **plaintiffs were paid $590 million:** William Alden, "KKR, Blackstone and TPG Private Equity Firms Agree to Settle Lawsuit on Collusion," *New York Times*, August 7, 2014; Thomas Heath, "Carlyle Settles Collusion Case for $115 Million," *Washington Post*, August 29, 2014.

72 **shareholders receive 40 percent lower premiums in club deals:** Micah Officer, O. Ozbas, and B. Sensoy, "Club Deals in Leveraged Buyouts," *J. Fin. Econ.* 98, no. 2 (2010), 214–40.

73 **in 2018, the share of deals involving two or more private equity firms:** Kevin Dowd, "The

Biggest Firms in Private Equity Are Clubbing Up Once Again."

73 **they have accounted for half of all private equity exits:** Reed Sherman, "Why Private Equity Has Jumped on the SPAC Boom of 2020," Breakout Point, December 28, 2020, https://tinyurl.com /365sxk8e.

75 **a lawsuit alleging cartel conduct by the company owning Bumble Bee tuna:** Mike Leonard, "Bumble Bee Parent Lion Capital Dragged Back into Antitrust Case," *Bloomberg Law*, March 22, 2022, https://tinyurl.com/mrzx9rtk.

76 **nine of the top private equity firms have themselves become public companies:** This ranking is based on ten private equity firms raising the greatest amount of funds in the Preqin league tables in 2021.

76 **Starting with KKR and Blackstone:** Blackstone, the massive private equity complex, is not the same as BlackRock, the massive index fund complex. BlackRock was founded in 1988 as a joint venture of Blackstone, but after the founders of the two firms (Stephen Schwarzman and Larry Fink, respectively) got into a dispute, Blackstone sold its interest in BlackRock and the two have not been affiliated since 1994.

78 **buyer and seller are both controlled by the same private**

164   **equity firm:** Ludovic Phalippou, "Beware of Venturing into Private Equity," *J. Econ. Persp.* 23 (2009), 147, 162–64 (overview of private equity conflicts).

78   **expense allocation:** In re Cherokee Investment Partners LLC and Cherokee Advisers LLC, Investment Advisers Act of 1940 Release No. 4258, Administrative Proceeding File No. 3-16945 (5 November 2015); In re First Reserve Management, LP, Investment Advisers Act of 1940 Release No. 4529, Administrative Proceeding File No. 3-17538 (September 14, 2016); In re Yucaipa Master Manager, LLC, Investment Adviser Act of 1940 Release No. 5074, Administrative Proceeding File No. 3-18930 (13 December 2018); In re Lincolnshire Management, Inc, Investment Advisers Act of 1940 Release No. 3927, Administrative Proceeding File No. 3-16139 (22 September 2014).

78   **deals between private equity firms and portfolio companies owned by their funds:** In re Centre Partners Management, LLC, Investment Advisers Act of 1940 Release No. 4604, Administrative Proceeding File No. 3-17764 (January 10, 2017).

78   **the expansion of private equity firms into other asset classes:** William A. Birdthistle and M. Todd Henderson, "One Hat Too Many? Investment Desegregation

in Private Equity," *U. Chi. L. Rev.* 76 (2009), 45.

78   **nearly all SEC private equity–related enforcement matters involve conflicts of interest:** Julie M. Riewe, Co-director of Asset Management Division, "Conflicts, Conflicts Everywhere," US Securities and Exchange Commission, February 26, 2015, https://www.sec.gov /news/speech/conflicts -everywhere-full-360-view. For examples of such enforcement cases, see Apollo Mgmt. V, L.P., Investment Advisors Act of 1940 Release No. 4493 (August 23, 2016); Blackstone Mgmt. Partners L.L.C., Investment Advisors Act of 1940 Release No. 4219 (October 7, 2015); In re Kohlberg Kravis Roberts & Co. L.P., Investment Advisers Act of 1940 Release No. 4131, Administrative Proceeding File No. 3-16656 (June 29, 2015).

79   **Clearlake Capital bought a growing cloud services firm:** Antoine Gara, "Clearlake, the U.S. Buyout Group Behind the Chelsea Bid," *Financial Times,* May 7, 2022; "ConvergeOne Agrees to Be Acquired by CVC Fund VII for $1.8 Billion," press release, November 7, 2018, https://tinyurl.com /2p939y5n.

80   **came growth in misbehavior:** These included an initial round under a Democratic administration in 2015 and 2016, but continued

under a Republican administration in 2018 and a new Democratic administration in 2021 and 2022. See, for instance, Apollo Mgmt. V, L.P., Investment Advisors Act of 1940 Release No. 4493 (August 23, 2016); Blackstone Mgmt. Partners L.L.C., Investment Advisors Act of 1940 Release No. 4219 (October 7, 2015); In re Kohlberg Kravis Roberts & Co. L.P., Investment Advisers Act of 1940 Release No. 4131, Administrative Proceeding File No. 3-16656 (June 29, 2015); In re Cherokee Investment Partners LLC and Cherokee Advisers LLC, Investment Advisers Act of 1940 Release No. 4258, Administrative Proceeding File No. 3-16945 (November 5, 2015). In re Yucaipa Master Manager, LLC, Investment Adviser Act of 1940 Release No. 5074, Administrative Proceeding File No. 3-18930 (December 13, 2018); *Securities and Exchange Commission v. Westport Capital Markets, LLC and Christopher E McClure*, Litigation Release No. 24007 (December 11, 2017); In re Potomac Asset Management Co, Inc and Goodloe E. Byron Jr., Investment Advisers Act of 1940 Release No. 4766, Administrative Proceeding File No. 3-18168 (September 11, 2017); Investment Advisers Act of 1940 Release No. 6049, Administrative Proceeding File No. 3-20900, In the Matter of Energy Capital Partners Management, LP (June 14, 2022) (failing to disclose disproportionate expense allocations to fund);

Investment Advisers Act of 1940 Release No. 5930, Administrative Proceeding File No. 3-20683, In the Matter of Global Infrastructure Management, LLC (December 20, 2021) (fee and expense disclosure failures).

81   **should not affect the value of a business, except due to market imperfections:** F. Modigliani and M. Miller, "The Cost of Capital, Corporation Finance and the Theory of Investment," *Am. Econ. Rev.* 48, no. 3 (1958), 261–97.

81   **Up to a point, debt is taxed more favorably than equity:** Since 1969, with tightened treatment adopted in 1982, if a company borrows so much money that its debt initially includes a "discount"—i.e., the funds it receives are lower than the face amount of the debt—then the tax code treats the discounted principal as interest, limiting the effective tax benefits of the debt. See 12 U.S.C. 1272; 26 CFR § 1.163-4.

81   **while dividends on equity are not:** As discussed more below, debt is said to address another market imperfection—the residual agency costs that arise when ownership and control separate (see chapter two). Debt is said to "discipline" managers by forcing them to pay out profits, rather than misusing it.

81   **the performance fee that is typically set at 20 percent of profits:** The additional

166   management fee, typically 2 percent
of assets under management, is
taxed normally as ordinary income.

**81   Capital gains on investments
are taxed more lightly than
ordinary income:** Tax rates in 2022
set the highest marginal rate on
long-term (over one year) capital
gains at 20 percent; the highest
marginal rate on ordinary income
and short-term capital gains is 37
percent, almost twice that for
long-term capital gains.

**82   management buyouts can be a
form of institutionalized insider
trading:** For example, F. P. Schadler
and J. E. Karns, "The Unethical
Exploitation of Shareholders in
Management Buyout
Transactions," *Journal of Business
Ethics* 9, no. 7 (1990), 595–602,
http://www.jstor.org/stable
/25072074.

**83   to sell portfolio companies at
industry peaks:** Oleg R. Gredil, "Do
Private Equity Managers Have
Superior Information on Public
Markets?" *Rev. Fin. Stud.* 57 (2022),
321–58.

**83   private equity backers since
the 1980s have told a different
story:** The classic "just so" story
was told by Michael C. Jensen,
"Agency Costs of Free Cash Flow,
Corporate Finance, and Takeovers,"
Am. Econ. Rev. 76 (1986), 323;
Michael C. Jensen, "Eclipse of the
Public Corporation," *Harvard

Business Review, September–
October 1989, 61.

**83   or even primarily because of
its tax advantages:** Steven Kaplan,
"The Effects of Management
Buyouts on Operating Performance
and Value," *J. Fin. Econ.* 24 (1989),
217, 217–18.

**83   adds incentives to increase
value, shared with managers who
co-invest:** Ronald W. Masulis and
Randall S. Thomas, "Does Private
Equity Create Wealth? The Effects
of Private Equity and Derivatives on
Corporate Governance," *U. Chi. L.
Rev.* 76 (2009), 219, 251-52.

**83   enables rapid interventions
to keep a company steady in
difficulties:** Francesca Cornelli and
Ōguzhan Karakas, "Private Equity
and Corporate Governance: Do
LBOs Have More Effective Boards?"
in *Globalization Of Alternative
Investments Working Papers Volume
1: The Global Economic Impact of
Private Equity Report 2008* (World
Economic Forum, 2008), 65, 72.

**84   by complacent, under-
incentivized managers:** Kaplan
and Strömberg, "Leveraged Buyouts
and Private Equity," p. 132 (noting
that in one study, "one-third of
[CEOs] . . . are replaced in the first
100 days while two-thirds are
replaced at some point over a
four-year period").

**84   once-thriving family
business hampered by nepotism:**

Nicholas Bloom, Raffaella Sadun, and John Van Reenen, "Do Private Equity Owned Firms Have Better Management Practices?" *Am. Econ. Rev.* 105 (2015), 442.

84 took his German shepherd along for a ride: Bryan Burrough and John Helyar, *Barbarians at the Gate: The Fall of RJR Nabisco* (1990); cf. Jesse Edgerton, "Agency Problems in Public Firms: Evidence from Corporate Jets in Leveraged Buyouts," *J. Fin.* 67 (2012), 2187 (public companies using corporate jets reduce their use after being acquired by private equity funds).

84 likely did improve value with better governance: Ronald J. Gilson and Jeffrey N. Gordon, "The Agency Costs of Agency Capitalism: Activist Investors and the Revaluation of Governance Rights," *Colum. L. Rev.* 113 (2013) 863, 889, 896.

84 today's public companies no longer resemble their predecessors: Nicholas Bloom, Raffaella Sadun, and John Van Reenen, "Do Private Equity Owned Firms Have Better Management Practices?" (finding management improvements at family-owned firms, but not public companies, after being bought by private equity firms). See Elisabeth de Fontenay, "Private Equity's Governance Advantage: A Requiem," *Boston U. L. Rev.* 99 (2019), 1095–1122 (private

equity's governance advantages over public companies have faded). Another change is that private equity firms no longer engage in exclusively control acquisitions, and increasingly take minority positions in target companies, reducing their ability to use the strong governance interventions characteristic of full LBOs.

84 that constantly monitor and pressure public companies to do precisely the kinds of things: Nickolay Gantchev, Oleg R. Gredil, and Chotibhak Jotikasthira, "Governance Under the Gun: Spillover Effects of Hedge Fund Activism," *Rev. Fin.* 1 (2018); Alon Brav et al, "Hedge Fund Activism, Corporate Governance, and Firm Performance," *J. Fin.* 63 (2008), 1729, 1731–32; Marcel Kahan and Edward B. Rock, "Hedge Funds in Corporate Governance and Corporate Control," *U. Pa. L. Rev.* 155 (2007), 1021, 1024–25, 1029–42.

85 "We are all Henry Kravis now": Steve Kaplan, "The Evolution of U.S. Corporate Governance: We Are All Henry Kravis Now," *J. Private Equity* (Fall 1997), 7–14.

85 private equity firms add managerial expertise to the companies they buy: Nicholas Bloom, Raffaella Sadun, and John Van Reenen, "Do Private Equity Owned Firms Have Better Management Practices?"

168 86 **creditworthiness and reputation (to creditors):** Cem Demiroglu and Christopher M. James, "The Role of Private Equity Group Reputation in LBO Financing," *J. Fin. Econ.* 96 (2010), 306.

86 **"incestuous":** Annie Zhao and Guhan Subramanian, "Go-Shops Revisited," *Harvard Law Review* 133 (2020), 1215.

86 **"appears to be cheap debt financing":** Elisabeth de Fontenay, "Private Equity Firms as Gatekeepers," *Rev. Banking and Fin. L.* 33 (2013), 115, 120–21 and Victoria Ivashina and Anna Kovner, "The Private Equity Advantage: Leveraged Buyout Firms and Relationship Banking," *Rev. Fin. Stud.* 24 (2011), 2462, 2462–63; Ulf Axelson, Tim Jenkinson, Per Stromberg, and Michael S. Weisbach, "Borrow Cheap, Buy High? The Determinants of Leverage and Pricing in Buyouts," *J. Fin.* 68 (2013), 2223; Jonathan B Cohn, Edith S. Hotchkiss, and Erin M. Towery, "Sources of Value Creation in Private Equity Buyouts of Private Firms," *Rev. of Fin.* 26, no. 2 (2022), 257–85; Edith S. Hotchkiss, David C. Smith, and Per Strömberg, "Private Equity and the Resolution of Financial Distress," *Rev. Corp. Fin. Stud.* 10, no. 4 (2021), 694–747.

87 **buyers included not only other banks:** Victoria Ivashina and Anna Kovner, "The Private Equity Advantage: Leveraged Buyout Firms and Relationship Banking," *Rev. Fin. Stud.* 24, no. 7 (July 2011), 2462–98; Victoria Ivashina, "Note on the Leveraged Loan Market," Harvard Business School Background Note 214–047 (October 2013).

87 **suggesting private equity firms never had an overall ability to outperform:** Viral V. Acharya, Julian Franks, and Henri Servaes, "Private Equity: Boom and Bust?" *J. Applied Corp. Fin.* 19 (2007), 44; Andrew Ang et al, "Estimating Private Equity Returns from Limited Partner Cash Flows," *J. Fin.* 73 (2018), 1751.

87 **they no longer do so, especially net of fees:** In addition to the studies summarized in the text, another line of research asks about why the persistence of private equity across funds has fallen over time. Cf. Reiner Braun, Tim Jenkinson, and Ingo Stoff, "How Persistent Is Private Equity Performance? Evidence from Deal-Level Data," *J. Fin. Econ.* 123 (2017), 273 ("past performance is a poor predictor of the future"), with Arthur Korteweg and Morten Sorensen, "Skill and Luck in Private Equity Performance," *J. Fin. Econ.* 124 (2017), 535 ("We find high long-term persistence [in private equity returns across funds but] [p]erformance is noisy . . . making it difficult for investors to identify the private equity funds with top

quartile expected future performance and leaving little investable persistence.").

88   even as private equity firms earned 6 percent per year in fees: Ludovic Phalippou and Oliver Gottschalg, "The Performance of Private Equity Funds," *Rev. Fin. Stud.* 22 (2009), 1747. See also Steven N. Kaplan and Annette Schoar, "Private Equity Performance: Returns, Persistence, and Capital Flows," *J. Fin.* 60 (2005), 1791–1823.

88   "returns have been roughly equal to those of public markets": Robert S. Harris, Tim Jenkinson, and Steven N. Kaplan, "How Do Private Equity Investments Perform Compared to Public Equity?" *J. Inv. Mgmt.* 14 (2016), 14.

89   fraud: "CEO of Private Equity Fund Sentenced to 97 Months for $133 Million Bank and Securities Fraud Scheme," Department of Justice, May 13, 2022, https://tinyurl.com/ywf6uf9h.

89   poor working conditions: Joan Verdon, "PetSmart's Private Equity Owners Dogged by Worker Rights Campaign," *Forbes*, December 16, 2021, https://tinyurl.com/yck78hre; See also Jonathan Cohn, Nicole Nestoriak, and Malcolm Wardlaw, "Private Equity Buyouts and Workplace Safety," *Rev. Fin. Stud.* 34 (October 2021), 4832–75 ("workplace injury rates

[decline] after private equity buyouts of publicly traded U.S. firms").

89   wage reductions: Gretchen Morgenson, "Working for Companies Owned by Well-Heeled Private-Equity Firms Can Mean Lower Wages for Employees," NBC News, October 9, 2021, https://tinyurl.com/2zkux8jt.

89   customer overcharges: Loren Adler, Kathleen Hannick, and Sobin Lee, "High Air Ambulance Charges Concentrated in Private Equity-Owned Carriers," Brookings, October 13, 2020, https://healthpolicy.usc.edu/brookings-schaeffer/high-air-ambulance-charges-concentrated-in-private-equity-owned-carriers/; Charlie Eaton, "Agile Predators: Private Equity and the Spread of Shareholder Value Strategies to US For-Profit Colleges," *Socio-Econ. Rev.* 20, no. 2 (2022), 791–815 (for-profit universities owned by private equity funds or which are public companies previously owned by private equity funds report "unusually high debts and low graduation rates for students"); Charlie Eaton, Sabrina T. Howell, and Constantine Yannelis, "When Investor Incentives and Consumer Interests Diverge: Private Equity in Higher Education," *Rev. of Fin. Stud.* 33, no. 9 (2020), 4024–60 ("private equity-owned schools better capture government aid [but a]fter buyouts, we observe lower

170   education inputs, graduation rates, loan repayment rates, and earnings among graduates").

89   **elder abuse:** Dylan Scott, "Private Equity Ownership Is Killing People at Nursing Homes: A New Study Describes the Human Toll of Private Equity Firms Buying Up Nursing Homes," Vox, February 22, 2021, https://tinyurl.com /54dy75kp.

89   **health-and-safety violations:** "Profit Over Safety: Private Equity's Leveraged Bet on Packers Sanitation," Private Equity Stakeholder Project, March 2022, https://tinyurl.com/2p884fb5.

89   **government corruption:** Danny Hakim, "Carlyle Settles with New York in Pension Case," *New York Times*, May 14, 2009; Mara Faccio and Hung-Chia Hsu, "Politically Connected Private Equity and Employment," *J. Fin.* 72, no. 2 (2017), 539–74 (finding job growth in electoral districts after buyouts by politically connected private equity firms, more so in election years and in states with high corruption). See also Todd C. Frankel, "The Search for Oligarchs' Wealth in U.S. Is Hindered by Investment Loopholes: Finding Yachts and Mansions Is Easier Than Uncovering Money in Private Equity Funds That Don't Need to Adopt Anti-corruption Rules, Experts Say," *Washington Post*, March 16, 2022.

89   **toxic emissions:** Aymeric Bellon, "Does Private Equity Ownership Make Firms Cleaner? The Role of Environmental Liability Risks," working paper, November 2021 (finding that private equity ownership reduced toxic emissions overall, but increased them at locations subject to weak environmental enforcement, such as on federal and Native American territories).

89   **greenhouse gas emissions:** For instance, Hiroko Tabuchi, "Private Equity Funds, Sensing Profit in Tumult, Are Propping Up Oil," *New York Times*, November 13, 2021; David Fickling, "Why Private Equity Won't Be the Savior of Fossil Fuels," FAMag, January 6, 2022, https://tinyurl.com/yjz9pf8v (arguing that private equity firms are reluctant to buy carbon-emitting businesses because they need to exit the investments to earn a profit, and expect multiples for such firms to fall due to transition risk).

89   **and even human rights abuses:** Selin Bucak, "Private Equity Funds May Come Under Increased Scrutiny for Failing to Prevent Human Rights Abuses by Portfolio Companies," CityWire, July 22, 2021, https://tinyurl.com /yke2w8dp (private equity–owned company's spyware was alleged to have been used by repressive regimes to invade privacy of journalists and rival politicians).

89   **where they have weak legal entitlements:** "Detailed Description of Employment Protection Legislation," OECD, 2019, https://tinyurl.com /tfm7ty45, and OECD, data https:// tinyurl.com/4rsve49r.

89   **underpriced unemployment insurance:** See Catherine R. Albiston and Catherine L. Fisk, "Precarious Work and Precarious Welfare: How the Pandemic Reveals Fundamental Flaws of the U.S. Social Safety Net," 42 Berkeley J. Emp. & Lab. L. 257 (2021).

91   **an important way that differential access to investment options concentrates wealth over time:** Romain Duval, "Heterogeneity and Persistence in Returns to Wealth," IMF Working Paper, July 2018.

91   **reduce employment and create significant levels of job turnover:** Steven J. Davis, John Haltiwanger, Kyle Handley, Ron Jarmin, Josh Lerner, and Javier Miranda, "Private Equity, Jobs, and Productivity," *Am. Econ. Rev.* 104, no. 12 (2014), 3956–90 ("target establishments experience deeper job losses after private equity buyouts than control establishments," buyouts produce both significant job destruction and job creation, with implied dislocation costs for many workers; "Gross job destruction at target establishments outpaces destruction at controls by a cumulative 10 percentage points over five years post buyout. Thus, pre-existing employment positions are at greater risk of loss in the wake of private equity buyouts."); Manfred Antoni, Ernst Maug, and Stefan Obernberger, "Private Equity and Human Capital Risk," *J. Fin. Econ.* 133, no. 3 (2019), 634–57 ("Buyouts are followed by a reduction in overall employment and an increase in employee turnover."); Mark Heil, "How Does Finance Influence Labour Market Outcomes? A Review of Empirical Studies," *J. Econ. Stud.* 47, no. 6 (2020), 1197–1232 ("Factors that may reduce employment include the effects of leveraged buyouts on acquired firms"); Martin Olsson and Joacim Tåg, "Are Foreign Private Equity Buyouts Bad for Workers?" *Econ. Ltrs.* 172(C) (2018), 1–4 (domestic but not cross-border buyouts reduce employment and wages).

91   **reduce hourly wages relative to revenues:** Steven J. Davis, John Haltiwanger, Kyle Handley, Ron Jarmin, Josh Lerner, and Javier Miranda, "Private Equity, Jobs, and Productivity," p. 3959 ("compared to control firms, target firms more aggressively close manufacturing plants in the lower part of the total factor productivity [TFP] distribution. They also open new plants in the upper part of the TFP distribution at nearly twice the rate of control firms, and they are

172   much less likely to open low productivity establishments"); Manfred Antoni, Ernst Maug, and Stefan Obernberger, "Private Equity and Human Capital Risk," ("Employees of buyout targets experience earnings declines equivalent to 2.8% of median earnings in the fifth year after the buyout."). Wage reductions (or slower wage growth) can be rebranded as "productivity improvements." Productivity is defined in "Private Equity, Jobs, and Productivity" as "output" less various "inputs," including "total hours of production and non-production workers." If hourly wages fall, while revenues remain flat or grow, productivity grows.

91   **destabilize communities that are dependent on durable jobs:** For example, Eileen Appelbaum, Written Testimony before the United States Senate Committee on Banking, Housing, and Urban Affairs Subcommittee on Economic Policy Hearing Entitled: Protecting Companies and Communities from Private Equity Abuse (October 20, 2021) (noting negative effect on communities of Toys "R" Us buyout and subsequent bankruptcy, which wiped out private equity fund investors, but still generated profits for KKR, Bain, and Vornado).

91   **depending on how shares are counted:** The very uncertainty about how much they own reflects the complex control and ownership that is typical of the publicly traded private equity firms. Carlyle's Annual Proxy Statement (p. 69) reports that its officers and directors as a group own 30 percent, but also reports that the Carlyle management company (in which the senior leaders also own the largest stakes) own 43 percent (inclusive of the 30 percent owned directly by the officers and directors). The 35 percent figure comes directly from an interview in *New York Times* of David Rubenstein, one of the founders and senior managers. A. R. Sorkin, "A Leadership Shakeup That Rattled Wall Street," Dealbook, September 3, 2022.

91   **public companies have moved in the same direction:** Lawrence Mishel and Julia Wolfe, "CEO Compensation Has Grown 940% Since 1978, Typical Worker Compensation Has Risen only 12% During That Time," Economic Policy Institute, August 14, 2019, https://tinyurl.com/yw2y4a4t.

91   **top earnings the US in law, sports, and investment banking:** Steven N. Kaplan and Joshua Rauh, "It's the Market: The Broad-Based Rise in the Return to Top Talent," *J. Econ. Persp.* (2013).

91   **has experienced massive increases in wealth disparities:** Thomas Piketty, *Capital in the Twenty-First Century* (2014).

92 **contribute to job polarization:** Martin Olsson and Joacim Tåg, "Private Equity, Layoffs, and Job Polarization," *J. of Labor Econ.* 35, no. 3 (2017), 697–754.

92 **attributes the explosion at the top of the US and UK income distribution:** Thomas Piketty, *Capital in the Twenty-First Century*, 332.

92 **as their defenders stress:** For instance, Douglas Holtz-Eakin, Testimony, Protecting Companies and Communities from Private Equity Abuse, United States Senate Committee on Banking, Housing, and Urban Affairs Subcommittee on Economic Policy (October 20, 2021).

CHAPTER FOUR

97 **or about one proposal at every forty-two US public companies:** Gerald F. Davis and Tracy A. Thompson, "A Social Movement Perspective on Corporate Control," *Adm. Sci. Q.* 39 (March 1994), 141–73.

97 **roughly one proposal for every eight companies:** June Hu, Melissa Sawyer, and Marc Treviño, "2022 Proxy Season Review: Rule 14a-8 Shareholder Proposals," Harvard Law School Forum on Corp. Gov., August 25, 2022; SEC Substantial Implementation, Duplication, and Resubmission of Shareholder Proposals Under Exchange Act Rule 14a-8, Release No. 34-95267 (September 12, 2022), https://www.sec.gov/rules /proposed/2022/34-95267.pdf (Table 2).

97 **"than in the entire history of shareholder proposals prior to 1990":** Jayne W. Barnard, "Institutional Investors and the New Corporate Governance," 69 *North Carolina Law Review* 1135, 1156 (1991).

97 **from 1 percent over the period from 2010 to 2019 to 12.4 percent in 2020:** Roberto Tallarita, "Stockholder Politics," *Hastings Law Journal* 73, no. 6 (2022), 1617, 1647.

97 **suggests how important growth in institutional ownership was from 1960 to 1990:** Political success from the late 1980s on for US institutional shareholders contrasts with their absence from debates over one federal law (the Williams Act) adopted in 1968 in response to an early, much less economically significant wave of takeovers, in the 1950s and 1960s. As noted by John Armour and David Skeel, no institutional shareholder agents spoke in congressional hearings on that law. John Armour and David A. Skeel Jr., "Who Writes the Rules for Hostile Takeovers, and Why?—The Peculiar Divergence of U.S. and U.K. Takeover Regulation August," *Geo. L. J.* 95 (2007), 1727. Instead, it was the SEC that defended shareholder

174   rights against lobbying by corporate managers. For instance, Full Disclosure of Corporate Equity Ownership and in Corporate Takeover Bids: Hearings on S. 510 Before the Subcomm, on Securities of the Comm. on Banking and Currency, 90th Cong. 43 (1967), at 178 (statement of Manuel Cohen, Chair, Securities and Exchange Commission).

100   **are initiated by organizations, not individuals:** Roberto Tallarita, "Stockholder Politics," pp. 1617, 1642 (Table 6), and 1661 (Table 9).

100   **conservative organizations have also brought hundreds of proposals:** National Center for Public Policy Research alone has filed more than a hundred proposals in recent years. Roberto Tallarita, "Stockholder Politics," p. 1663.

100   **diversity, climate change, and corporate political activity:** Roberto Tallarita, "Stockholder Politics," p. 1634.

101   **concern a litany of modern political issues:** Roberto Tallarita, "Stockholder Politics," p. 1635.

101   **publicly pursued diversity as one of its own corporate goals:** For State Street's gender diversity policy, see https://tinyurl.com /yc4kskdk.

101   **directly opposite the New York Stock Exchange:** The statue has not been received uniformly by commentators. For instance, Christine Emba, "'Fearless Girl' and 'Charging Bull' Are More Alike Than You'd Think," *Washington Post*, April 14, 2017; Jillian Jorgensen, "Letitia James Wants Fearless Girl to Be Permanent," *Daily News*, May 13, 2017.

102   **can also be found on its public-facing website:** https:// www.statestreet.com/values /inclusion-diversity/diversity -goals.html.

102   **It reports 220 corporate "engagements" on the topic:** See https://tinyurl.com/2p8d3dbb. Vanguard similarly reports "581 engagements related to diversity (up from 198 the previous year)," https://tinyurl.com/bdf3xm8f.

102   **has published diversity guidelines expecting "all companies in our portfolio":** "Guidance on Diversity Disclosures and Practices," State Street, January 2022, https://tinyurl.com /2mfxtpkz.

103   **board diversity practices have significantly increased in recent years:** "Report: Disclosure of US Board Diversity Soars; Boards Increase Gender Diversity Faster Than Racial and Ethnic Diversity," The Conference Board, press

release, October 19, 2021, https://tinyurl.com/28kj32t2.

103 **there is a compelling business case for increased diversity on corporate boards:** For instance, Paul Gompers and Silpa Kovvali, "The Other Diversity Dividend," *Harvard Business Review* 72, July–August 2018; Cedric Herring, "Does Diversity Pay? Race, Gender, and the Business Case for Diversity," *Am. Soc. Rev.* 74, no. 2 (2009), 208; David Rock and Heidi Grant, "Why Diverse Teams Are Smarter," *Harvard Business Review*, November 4, 2016; Stephanie J. Creary, Mary-Hunter ("Mae") McDonnell, Sakshi Ghai, and Jared Scruggs, "When and Why Diversity Improves Your Board's Performance," *Harvard Business Review*, March 27, 2019; See also G. Bernile, V. Bhagwat, and S. Yonker, "Board Diversity, Firm Risk, and Corporate Policies," *J. Fin. Econ.* 127 (2018), 588–612 ("greater board diversity leads to lower volatility and better performance"); M. Nadeem, T. Suleman, and A. Ahmed, "Women on Boards, Firm Risk and the Profitability Nexus," *Int'l Rev. of Econ. & Fin.* 64 (2019), 427–42 ("positive impact of [women on boards] and firm risk on profitability"); O. Kuzmina and V. Melentyeva, "Gender Diversity in Corporate Boards: Evidence from Quota-Implied Discontinuities," working paper, 2021 ("having more women on corporate boards has large positive effects on Tobin's Q [value] and buy-and-hold returns").

104 **"Carlyle portfolio companies with two or more diverse board members":** Jason M. Thomas and Megan Starr, "From Impact Investing to Investing for Impact," The Carlyle Group, 2020, https://www.carlyle.com/sites/default/files/2020-02/From%20Impact%20Investing%20to%20Investing%20for%20Impact_022420.pdf.

104 **whether they have a diverse board, or explain why not:** See https://tinyurl.com/2nunrz2c.

104 **"progressive social engineering":** For example, David Burton "Nasdaq's Proposed Board-Diversity Rule Is Immoral and Has No Basis in Economics," *Heritage Foundation Blog*, March 9, 2021; Richard Morrison, "Nasdaq's Board Diversity Rule Still a Mistake," *Competitive Enterprise Institute Blog*, August 10, 2021; Pat Toomey, "Statement on the SEC's Approval of NASDAQ's Board Diversity Requirements," August 6, 2021; Jesse M. Fried, "Will Nasdaq's Diversity Rules Harm Investors?" 12 *Harv. Bus. L. Rev.* Online, art. 1, 2021, at 1. Illustrating the politicized op-ed-like nature of these responses, Fried relies on studies of Norway's board diversity mandate, as if it were probative of the

176   Nasdaq's comply-or-explain standard, and does not cite studies showing that comply-or-explain board rules have better effects than mandates. Larry Fauver et al., "Board Reforms and Firm Value: Worldwide Evidence," *J. Fin. Econ.* 125 (2017), 120 (finding greater increase in firm value from comply-or-explain-based reforms than for rule-based corporate board reforms on firm value across forty-one countries). He says the most recent study of the Norway mandate simply "question[ed] the magnitude of some of these results," when in fact that study, B. Espen Eckbo et al., "Valuation Effects of Norway's Board Gender-Quota Law Revisited," *Man. Sci.* 68, no. 6 (2022), 4112–34, found the "valuation effect of Norway's quota law was statistically insignificant." Fried cites studies finding a negative effect of a California board diversity mandate, but fails to note that one he claims finds the mandate caused negative effects in fact attributes the negative effect to a broader signal about state politics and not about the mandate itself. Felix von Meyerinck, Alexandra Niessen-Ruenzi, Markus Schmid, and Steven Davidoff Solomon, "As California Goes, So Goes the Nation," *SSRN*, August 31, 2021, https://ssrn.com/abstract =3303798. Fried asserts the Nasdaq "ignores" what he characterizes as "the bottom line" of another study, Renée B. Adams and Daniel

Ferreira, "Women in the Boardroom and Their Impact on Governance and Performance," *J. Fin. Econ.* 94 (2009), 291, in which Fried says "the average effect of gender diversity on firm performance is negative." However, Nasdaq not only acknowledged the study in its proposal, but noted it found that diversity could have "detrimental effects in companies with strong shareholder rights." (See https://tinyurl.com/2nunrz2c.) Fried does not note that the SEC's approval order cites the same study, and summarizes it correctly: "This study observes that the effect of gender diversity on firm performance may be negative and in general depends on the specification of the analysis," https://tinyurl.com/ym75tv43. Fried's "bottom line" is taken from the study's abstract, and does not fairly capture the study's overall findings. Those findings include a key specification designed to control for endogeneity, one of the primary bases on which the authors critique earlier studies. In that specification, the average effect is negative, but not statistically significant—scientifically equivalent to zero. The actual "bottom line" of the study, in other words, is mixed, with some positive findings, some negative, and some zero.

104   **nearly twenty red-state state attorneys general:** Cozen

O'Connor, "Diversity or Discrimination? Amicus Brief Argues Against Nasdaq's Board Diversity Rule," JDSupra, January 7, 2022, https://www.jdsupra.com /legalnews/diversity-or -discrimination-amicus-2635144/.

105 **"freedom for private actors like the stock exchanges to innovate":** For amicus brief, see https://tinyurl.com/2subpchz.

105 **Vanguard, BlackRock, and State Street:** Nasdaq Stock Mkt. LLC, Response to Comments and Notice of Filing of Amendment No. 1 of Proposed Rule Change to Adopt Listing Rules Related to Board Diversity (February 26, 2021), at 12. However, consistent with the index funds dividing over the details of how to approach issues, only State Street filed a comment letter specifically supporting the standard.

105 **"Return-seeking investors have different interests around these proposed rules":** Jesse M. Fried, "Will Nasdaq's Diversity Rules Harm Investors?"

106 **written in 1971 for the Chamber of Commerce:** Memorandum to Eugene B. Sydnor Jr. from Lewis F. Powell Jr., Education Committee Chairman, US Chamber of Commerce (August 23, 1971), https://tinyurl.com /bdhkr2vm.

106 **proposed boiling down campaign finance regulation:** George F. Will, "Let's Play 20 Questions," *Newsweek*, March 15, 1999.

107 **"allows consenting adults to give as much as they want to whomever they want":** "McCain's Future," *Wall Street Journal*, March 10, 2000. See Norman Ornstein, "Full Disclosure: The Dramatic Turn Away from Campaign Transparency," *New Republic*, May 7, 2011.

107 **unashamedly reversed their commitment to disclosure:** George F. Will, "Let Us Disclose That Free-Speech Limits Are Harmful," *Washington Post*, July 11, 2010.

107 **Ultimately, Congress failed to act:** John C. Coates and Taylor Lincoln, "Fulfilling the Promise of 'Citizens United,'" *Washington Post*, September 6, 2011, and related white paper, available at https:// ssrn.com/abstract=1923804.

108 **served in political positions after retiring:** John C. Coates, "Corporate Politics, Governance, and Value Before and After *Citizens United*," *Journal of Empirical Legal Studies* 9 (2012), 657–96.

108 **a distraction for senior managers from ordinary business:** Lucian Bebchuk and Robert J. Jackson, "Corporate Political

178   Speech: Who Decides?" *Harv. L. Rev.* 124 (2010), 83–117; Paul K. Chaney, Mara Faccio, and David Parsley, "The Quality of Accounting Information in Politically Connected Firms," *J. Acc't & Econ.* 51 (2011), 58–76; Mara Faccio, "Differences Between Politically Connected and Non-Connected Firms: A Cross-Country Analysis," *Fin. Mgt.* 39 (2010), 905–27; Mara Faccio, Ronald W. Masulis, and John J. McConnell, "Political Connections and Corporate Bailouts," *J. Fin.* 56 (2006) 2597–2635; Michael Hadani and D. Schuler, "In Search of El Dorado: The Elusive Financial Returns on Corporate Political Investments," *Str. Mgt. J.* 34 (2013), 165–81; Rajesh Aggarwal, Felix Meschke, and Tracy Yue Wang, "Corporate Political Donations: Investment or Agency?" *Bus. and Politics* 14, no. 1 (2012); Jin-Hyuk Kim, "Corporate Lobbying Revisited," *Bus. and Politics* 10, no. 2 (2008).

108   **in which they pledged to disclose their electioneering activities:** "2020 CPA-Zicklin Index of Corporate Political Disclosure and Accountability," Center for Political Accountability, https://tinyurl.com/6yt4vr23.

108   **the average support level was 41 percent—all-time highs:** "2022 Proxy Season Review: Part 1," Sullivan and Cromwell, LLP, August 8, 2022, https://tinyurl.com/3dmdh65w.

109   **had supported a standard disclosure resolution:** "2019 Proxy Season Analysis," CPA, December 17, 2019, https://tinyurl.com/3zyzfrpf.

109   **contrasts with support from other institutions:** "Corporate Governance Policies," Council of Institutional Investors, March 7, 2022, https://www.cii.org/files/03_07_22_corp_gov_policies.pdf.

109   **BlackRock and Vanguard backed the Center for Political Accountability's model disclosure proposal:** "2019 Proxy Season Analysis."

110   **but Flowers changed nothing about its political disclosures:** "Voting Insight: Corporate Political Activity Shareholder Proposal at Flowers Foods," Vanguard Investment Stewardship Insights, July 2022.

111   **which in the 2022 election cycle gave more than $1 million:** Analysis of Investment Company Institute, Open Secrets, https://tinyurl.com/277ebvjz.

111   **more lobbyists than the institute:** Open Secrets, https://www.opensecrets.org/federal-lobbying.

112   **BlackRock's representatives were loud critics of the scholarship:** BlackRock has used data tricks to minimize the growing

scale of index fund ownership, for example. See, for example, https://corpgov.law.harvard.edu/2019/07/17/shareholders-are-dispersed-and-diverse/ (presenting data on ownership by index fund complexes of total world equity market capitalization, which distorts the actual share of ownership of the largest US companies, by including companies of smaller size and in geographic regions where index funds have lower but growing market share). In another example, the author listened as an index fund industry representative critiqued one academic paper claiming antitrust harms, and then, thirty minutes later, having heard the author's responses—which while not conclusive on the overall topic did convincingly repudiate some of the ways in which the critique had used "straw man" mischaracterizations of the work—repeated the same critiques as if the author had never responded.

112 **BlackRock attended conferences:** For instance, http://www.law.harvard.edu/faculty/bebchuk/Harvard-Law-School.mp4.

112 **published white papers:** For instance, https://corpgov.law.harvard.edu/2019/08/07/diversified-portfolios-do-not-reduce-competition/; https://tinyurl.com/5bvvek2a; https://tinyurl.com/bdzbkwch.

112 **hired lobbyists to meet with politicians:** For instance, https://tinyurl.com/ycxnkyu2 (disclosure by BlackRock registered lobbyist meeting with council to Senate Banking Committee regarding the S. 1811, Merger Enforcement Improvement Act, which would have required the FTC to study the effects of common ownership on competition).

112 **"Who Cares Wins":** "Who Cares Wins: Connecting Financial Markets to a Changing World," https://tinyurl.com/2nt6dcsx. Endorsers included ABN Amro, AXA, Banco do Brasil, BNP Paribas, Credit Suisse, Deutsche Bank, Goldman Sachs, HSBC, Morgan Stanley, and UBS.

112 **the South Africa divestment movement of the 1980s:** "Disinvestment from South Africa: They Did Well by Doing Good," *Contemp. Econ. Pol'y* 15, no. 1 (January 1997), 76–86. The Heritage Foundation labeled this movement "coercive" and motivated by "vengeance." "For US Firms in South Africa, the Threat of Coercive Sullivan Principles," Heritage Foundation, November 12, 1984; "The Choice for U.S. Policy in South Africa: Reform or Vengeance," Heritage Foundation, July 25, 1986. To date, Heritage has not condemned efforts by the oil and gas industry to persuade Texas and West Virginia to stop doing business with BlackRock.

180   112   **but became more widespread in the 1990s:** Christopher Geczy, Robert F. Stambaugh, and David Levin, "Investing in Socially Responsible Mutual Funds," *Rev. of Asset Pricing Stud.* 11, no. 2 (2021), 309–51.

113   **"one-year growth rate of ESG fund launches":** Tania Lynn Taylor and Sean Collins, "Ingraining sustainability in the next era of ESG investing," Deloitte Insights, April 5, 2022, https://tinyurl.com /3ettetyz.

113   **generate immediate media coverage:** For example, Andrew Ross Sorkin, "BlackRock's Message: Contribute to Society, or Risk Losing Our Support," *New York Times*, January 15, 2018.

113   **his views are analyzed carefully by the investment community:** Business professors publish columns about the letters, such as, Knut Haanaes and Paul Strebel, "The BlackRock Letter: A Turning Point for Real Change? A Strong Endorsement of the Emergence of a Serious Approach to Sustainability," IMD, February 2018, https://tinyurl.com /mptwz92u, as do law firms, such as Paul A. Davies, Michael D. Green, and James Bee, "BlackRock 2022 Letter to CEOs Highlights the Importance of Sustainability," Latham & Watkins LLP, February 16, 2022, https://tinyurl.com /4mcxn9js.

113   **"Capitalism has the power to shape society and act as a powerful catalyst for change":** Larry Fink, "The Power of Capitalism," 2022 Letter to CEOs, blackrock.com/corporate/investor -relations/larry-fink-ceo-letter.

113   **"also show how it makes a positive contribution to society":** Larry Fink, "Annual Letter to CEOs: A Sense of Purpose," January 12, 2018, https://tinyurl.com /459235v6.

113   **"climate risk is investment risk":** Larry Fink, "A Fundamental Reshaping of Finance," 2020 Letter to CEOs, blackrock.com/us /individual/larry-fink-ceo-letter.

114   **pending rule proposal on climate-related disclosure:** Securities and Exchange Commission, Enhancement and Standardization of Climate-Related Disclosures for Investors, Rel. Nos. 33-11042; 34-94478 (March 21, 2022), https://tinyurl.com /ur6345v4.

114   **BlackRock filed a twenty-two-page comment letter:** BlackRock Letter, June 17, 2022. https://www.blackrock.com /corporate/literature/publication /sec-enhancement-and -standardization-of-climate -related-disclosures-for -investors-061722.pdf.

115   **"exceed[s] the bounds of the SEC's lawful authority":** Letter

from US Chamber of Commerce to Vanessa A. Countryman, Secretary, US Securities and Exchange Commission, June 16, 2022, https://tinyurl.com/37seucxt.

115 goes beyond the SEC's constitutional authority: Letter from Continental Resources to Gary Gensler, Chairman, Securities and Exchange Commission, June 17, 2922, https://tinyurl.com/78ck8w8p.

115 Occidental Petroleum's comment letter states: Letter from Occidental Petroleum Corporation to Vanessa A. Countryman, Secretary, US Securities and Exchange Commission, June 17, 2022, https://tinyurl.com/4xnbxybh. See supportive letters from Microsoft, Uber, at https://www.sec.gov/comments/s7-10-22/s71022.htm.

115 "BlackRock had gone too far in pushing an environmental agenda": Angel Au-Yeung, "The 70 BlackRock Analysts Who Speak for Millions of Shareholders," *Wall Street Journal*, June 18, 2022.

115 attributed the drop to the specifics of the proposals: Angel Au-Yeung, "The 70 BlackRock Analysts Who Speak for Millions of Shareholders."

116 climate change is a real threat: Andrew Ross Sorkin, Vivian Giang, Stephen Gandel, Bernhard

Warner, Michael J. de la Merced, Lauren Hirsch, and Ephrat Livni, "BlackRock Seeks to Defend Its Reputation Over E.S.G. Fight," *New York Times*, September 8, 2022, https://www.nytimes.com/2022/09/08/business/dealbook/blackrock-texas-defend-reputation-esg-fight.html; for BlackRock's response, see https://tinyurl.com/mryb4ear.

116 while also providing political cover: Letter from Vanguard to Vanessa A. Countryman, Secretary, US Securities and Exchange Commission, June 16, 2022, p. 2, https://tinyurl.com/37seucxt ("The Proposed Rules should not mandate that companies disclose climate-related information that is not material.").

117 which is based on data from Open Secrets: Open Secrets groups private equity and investment firms in its tracking, but of the top ten sources of contributions identified in the category, eight self-identify as private equity firms, and of the five largest individual lobbying clients, four are private equity firms, so the bulk of tracked political contributions are in fact private equity and not other kinds of investment firms (family offices, early-stage venture capital, or hedge funds, for example), as Open Secrets confirms: "So-called private equity companies, which make billions of dollars investing individuals' and institutions'

182   money in private companies, make up the largest segment of this category," https://www .opensecrets.org/industries/indus .php?ind=F2600.

118   **"private equity and hedge fund industries [have] pour[ed] nearly $347.7 million into 2022 midterms":** Taylor Giorno and Srijita Datta, "Private Equity and Hedge Fund Industries Pour Nearly $347.7 Million into 2022 Midterms," Open Secrets, September 7, 2022, https://tinyurl .com/mu3599nm.

119   **who was only willing to vote for the law if the carried interest reform was deleted:** Aime Williams and Caitlin Gilbert, "Kyrsten Sinema Is Significant Beneficiary of Private Equity Lobbying Machine," *Financial Times*, August 7, 2022 ("Sinema's assent came with a notable proviso: scrapping the promise to end a notorious tax loophole allowing private equity and hedge fund managers to lower their tax bills.").

119   **"Blackstone Group has given the most money to Sinema's political operation":** Taylor Giorno and Srijita Datta, "Private Equity and Hedge Fund Industries Pour Nearly $347.7 Million into 2022 Midterms."

120   **Envision, owned by KKR, and TeamHealth, owned by Blackstone, were behind this dark-money campaign:** Eileen Appelbaum, "A Surprise Ending for Surprise Billing? Compromise Legislation to End the Practice Has Private Equity Firms Nervous," *American Prospect*, December 16, 2020; Margot Sanger-Katz, Julie Creswell, and Reed Abelson, "Mystery Solved: Private-Equity-Backed Firms Are Behind Ad Blitz on 'Surprise Billing': Two Doctor-Staffing Companies Are Pushing Back Against Legislation that Could Hit Their Bottom Lines," *New York Times*, September 13, 2019, updated September 30, 2021.

120   **"Our new name better conveys what private equity is all about: growing companies":** Peter Lattman, "Private Equity's Makeover Effort Starts with Trade Group," *New York Times*, September 14, 2010, https:// archive.nytimes.com/dealbook .nytimes.com/2010/09/14/private -equitys-makeover-effort-starts -with-trade-group/.

120   **"I think we get off on the wrong track by the name 'private equity'":** Peter Lattman, "Private Equity's Makeover Effort Starts with Trade Group."

121   **in 2022, it spent more than $2.9 million on lobbying:** LDA Reports, United States Senate (2012, 2022).

121   **"data on private equity investment's impact on employment in the US is anecdotal":** Douglas Lowenstein, Testimony before House Financial Services Committee, May 16, 2007, https://tinyurl.com/skpupers.

121   **"America for Sale? An Examination of the Practices of Private Funds":** Drew Maloney, Testimony before the U.S. House Financial Services Committee "America for Sale? An Examination of the Practices of Private Funds," November 19, 2019.

121   **KKR was caught misrepresenting the effects of its buyouts:** "Advocates of More Big LBOs Hit with Some Big Hard Facts," *St. Louis Post-Dispatch*, June 4, 1989 ("a widely quoted economic study by [KKR relied on] projected . . . numbers . . . [but] the word 'projected' is conspicuously absent from the KKR study").

121   **pays for research reports touting the industry's contribution to employment:** "Economic contribution of the US private equity sector in 2020," Ernst & Young, Prepared for the American Investment Council, May 2021.

121   **has opposed draft legislation aimed at regulating private equity:** Charles Swenson, "Economic Impact Analysis of the Stop Wall Street Looting Act (S.2155/H.R. 3848)," Center for Capital Markets, November 12, 2019, https://tinyurl.com/2s38svp9.

122   **also sponsors research and roundtables on the industry:** Institute for Private Capital research page, https://uncipc.org/index.php/research/.

122   **perform an unusually high number of well-reimbursed procedures and bill high amounts to Medicare:** Katie Hafner, "Why Private Equity Is Furious Over a Paper in a Dermatology Journal," *New York Times*, October 26, 2018. The article was S. Konda, J. Francis, K. Motaparthi, and J. M. Grant-Kels, "Corporatization and Private Equity in Dermatology, Future Considerations for Clinical Dermatology in the Setting of 21st Century American Policy Reform: Corporatization and the Rise of Private Equity in Dermatology," *J. of the Am. Acad. of Dermatology*, 2018.

122   **such investors "are placing greater emphasis on diversity":** Kem Ihenacho, Clare Scott, and Anne Mainwaring, Latham & Watkins LLP, "PE Firms Poised for Diversity Drive," The Harvard Law School Forum on Corporate Governance, August 15, 2022, https://corpgov.law.harvard.edu/2022/08/15/pe-firms-poised-for-diversity-drive/.

184   123   **attempted to develop forms of self-regulation on a range of issues:** Eilis Ferran, "The Regulation of Hedge Funds and Private Equity: A Case Study in the Development of the EU's Regulatory Response to the Financial Crisis," working paper, 2011, https://ssrn.com/abstract =1762119.

123   **Both Carlyle and KKR started voluntarily publishing sustainability reports:** See https://www.carlyle.com/impact /esg-report-archive; https://www .kkr.com/responsibility /sustainable-investing.

123   **"factor ESG into their investment decisions":** Robert G. Eccles, Vinay Shandal, David Young, and Benedicte Montgomery, "Private Equity Should Take the Lead in Sustainability," *Harvard Business Review*, July–August 2022 (citing survey by INSEAD's Global Private Equity Initiative).

124   **Red state politicians are beginning to impose their own legal requirements:** Angel Au-Yeung, "The 70 BlackRock Analysts Who Speak for Millions of Shareholders."

124   **accused the firm of prioritizing its climate agenda over pensioners' investments:** Andrew Ross Sorkin, Vivian Giang, Stephen Gandel, Bernhard Warner,

Michael J. de la Merced, Lauren Hirsch, and Ephrat Livni, "BlackRock Seeks to Defend Its Reputation Over E.S.G. Fight," *New York Times*, September 8, 2022.

124   **because they consider the firm to be too focused on environmental issues:** David Gilles, "How Republicans Are 'Weaponizing' Public Office Against Climate Action," *New York Times*, August 5, 2022.

124   **banned state pension funds from screening for climate and other ESG risks:** Danielle Moran, "DeSantis Amps Up ESG Attack, Banning Strategy for State Pensions," *Bloomberg Law*, August 23, 2022.

125   **that politicians use to raise funds and build popular support:** Andrew Petillon, "The Republican War on 'Woke Capitalism' Is Really Just a War on Capitalism: What the GOP's Hollow Attacks on ESG Investing Are Really About," *Slate*, June 23, 2022.

125   **Mike Pence was an early attacker of "woke capitalism":** Mike Pence, "Republicans Can Stop ESG Political Bias," *Wall Street Journal*, May 26, 2022; Ross Douthat, "The Rise of Woke Capital" February 28, 2018.

125   **"Why are woke CEOs using ESG to DESTROY our free**

market?": March 18, 2022, https://tinyurl.com/yc5pa8by.

125 **threatening an antitrust action of some kind in retaliation:** Press release, July 14, 2022, https://tinyurl.com/bddzrjhd.

125 **"We have a new bunch of emperors, and they're the people who vote the shares in the index funds":** https://www.wsj.com/articles/charlie-munger-expects-index-funds-to-change-the-worldand-not-in-a-good-way-11645055334?

126 **"locusts," "asset strippers," "casino capitalists," and "predators":** Douglas Cumming and Simona Zambelli, "Private Equity Performance Under Extreme Regulation," *J. Banking & Fin.* 37:5 (2013), 1508–23, citing J. A. Scharfman, *Private Equity Operational Due Diligence: Tools to Evaluate Liquidity, Valuation, and Documentation* (2012); Charlie Eaton, "Agile Predators: Private Equity and the Spread of Shareholder Value Strategies to US For-Profit Colleges," *Socio-Econ. Rev.* 20, no. 2 (2022), 791–815.

126 **are in the crosshairs of some members of the Democratic leadership:** Alan Rappeport and Emily Flitter, "Carried Interest Is Back in the Headlines. What Would a New Tax Proposal Do?" *New York Times,* July 28, 2022, https://www.nytimes.com/2022/07/28/business/carried-interest-loophole-tax-proposal.html?te=1&nl=the-morning&emc=edit_nn_20220729.

126 **increasing demands for information from public pension funds:** William W. Clayton, "Public Investors, Private Funds, and State Law," *Baylor Law Review* 72 (2020), 294.

126 **attack private equity on an investment basis, too:** Ludovic Phalippou & Oliver Gottschalg, "The Performance of Private Equity Funds," 22 Rev. Fin. Stud. 1747 (2009); Steven N. Kaplan, S. and Annette Schoar, "Private Equity Performance: Returns, Persistence, and Capital Flows," 60 J. Fin. 1791–1823 (2005); Erik Stafford, "Replicating Private Equity with Value Investing, Homemade Leverage, and Hold-to-Maturity Accounting," https://tinyurl.com/6zmu2drc, later published as "Replicating Private Equity with Value Investing, Homemade Leverage, and Hold-to-Maturity Accounting," 35:1 Rev. Fin. Stud. 299-342 (Jan. 2022); Robert S. Harris, Tim Jenkinson & Steven N. Kaplan, "How Do Private Equity Investments Perform Compared to Public Equity?," 14 J. Inv. Mgmt. 14 (2016); Farhad Manjoo, "Private Equity Doesn't Want You to Read This," *New York Times* (August 4, 2022).

186   126   **that the SEC had begun focusing on the private equity industry:** Andrew J Bowden, director of OCIE, "Spreading Sunshine in Private Equity," May 6, 2014, https://tinyurl.com/yckhw8z7.

126   **Similar public messaging from the SEC followed in 2015 and 2016:** Julie M Riewe, Co-director of Asset Management Division, "Conflicts, Conflicts Everywhere," February 16, 2015; Marc Wyatt, Acting Director of OCIE, "Private Equity: A Look Back and a Glimpse Ahead," May 13, 2015, https://tinyurl.com/nvrmyszv; Andrew Ceresney, Director of Division of Enforcement, Securities Enforcement Forum West 2016 Keynote Address: Private Equity Enforcement, May 12, 2016, https://tinyurl.com/2p9evm7x.

126   **the SEC has proposed requiring disclosure by private equity funds:** For the proposed rule, see https://www.sec.gov/rules/proposed/2022/ia-5955.pdf.

126   **a trend of increasing public disclosure obligations on private funds:** Steven Baker, et al, "The Trend of Increasing Disclosure Obligations for Private Funds Continues in 2022," Proskauer Rose LLP, https://tinyurl.com/5n6vjxjc.

126   **would impose transparency on the largest companies owned by private equity funds:** S.B. 4857, https://tinyurl.com/3ftbumnn.

127   **the potential negative effects of buyouts on acquired companies:** For example, Andreas Heed, "Regulation of Private Equity," J. Banking Reg. 12 (2010), 24 (discussing private equity's potential effects on banks amid financial crises).

127   **"Stop Wall Street Looting Act":** https://www.warren.senate.gov/newsroom/press-releases/warren-baldwin-brown-pocan-jayapal-colleagues-reintroduce-bold-legislation-to-fundamentally-reform-the-private-equity-industry.

127   **End the immunity of private equity firms from liability when portfolio companies break the law:** Pub.L. 100–379, Statutes at Large, 102 Stat. 890, codified at 29 U.S.C. §§ 2101–2109.

127   **have questioned a British company's plan to sell its baby formula unit to a buyout fund:** Stefania Palma, "Democrats Question Reckitt Benckiser's Plan to Sell Baby Formula Unit," *Financial Times*, June 22, 2022.

127   **Antitrust concerns overlap with these broader attacks:** Antoine Gara, "The Private Equity Club: How Corporate Raiders Became Teams of Rivals: The Industry Was Founded by Mercenary Dealmakers Who Bludgeoned Opponents. But Firms Now Nurture Complex Relationships with Their

Competitors," *Financial Times*, August 9, 2022.

128   Biden administration is reportedly taking on private equity: Stefania Palma, "US Trustbusters: Why Joe Biden Is Taking on Private Equity," *Financial Times*, August 22, 2022.

128   the antitrust effects of roll-ups in specific sectors, such as hospitals and data centers: Stefania Palma and James Fontanella-Khan, "Crackdown on Buyout Deals Coming, Warns Top US Antitrust Enforcer. Jonathan Kanter Fears Hollowing Out of American Economy Amid Private Equity Acquisition Spree," *Financial Times*, May 19, 2022.

CHAPTER FIVE

131   raw return data show a decline over time in private equity's ability to generate value: Heather Gillers and Dion Rabouin, "Pensions Brace for Private-Equity Losses," *Wall Street Journal*, September 24, 2022 (reporting that private equity "investments have outperformed stocks over the very long term, according to a private-equity index maintained by the data analytics firm Burgiss that doesn't include venture capital," but also that "over the ten years ended June 30, 2021, the yield [on private equity investments] was the same as the S&P 500, 14.8%").

133   "It will be interesting to see how far those at the top are willing to pull back the veil": Charles Duhigg, "Can Private Equity Build a Public Face?" *New York Times*, December 24, 2006.

134   capital is now mostly raised from other institutions: See note in chapter three, detailing data on pension fund beneficiaries.

137   the SEC could also require fund advisors to disclose in more detail how they go about fulfilling their fiduciary obligations: To the extent the SEC believes it needs more authority to require any of the foregoing that it believes in the best interest of investors, Congress should provide that authority.

140   Public comments commonly result in proposed rules being formally withdrawn: For instance, see Jason Webb Yackee and Susan Webb Yackee, "Testing the Ossification Thesis: An Empirical Examination of Federal Regulatory Volume and Speed, 1950–1990," *Geo. Wash. L. Rev.* 80 (2012), 1414 (Table 1, showing average proposed rules by Department of Interior over decades exceeding final rules by 10 percent or more); Jane E. Carmody, "To Withdraw or Not to Withdraw: Reviewability of an Agency's Withdrawn Proposed Rule," *Wash. L. Rev.* 93 (2018), 2107 (discussing whether common fact of rule withdrawals should be subject to judicial review).

188   140   **mitigates the risks associated with all-or-nothing decisions by individuals:** See Thomas Sowell, *Knowledge and Decisions* (1980), p. 382 ("The danger to the Constitution is not so much in particular laws as in the general climate of opinion in which law and government are no longer seen as a framework within which individuals make changes incrementally, but as themselves means of making categorical changes directly, according to the preferences of whoever happens to have control of those institutions.").